HAUNTED
RICHMOND

HAUNTED RICHMOND
THE SHADOWS OF SHOCKOE

SCOTT BERGMAN AND SANDI BERGMAN

Published by Haunted America
A Division of The History Press
Charleston, SC 29403
www.historypress.net

Copyright © 2007 by Scott Bergman and Sandi Bergman
All rights reserved

Cover image: Bellevue Elementary School. *Photo by Jon Hood.*

First published 2007
Second printing 2008
Third printing 2011
Fourth printing 2013

Manufactured in the United States

ISBN 978.1.59629.320.5

Library of Congress Cataloging-in-Publication Data

Bergman, Scott.
Haunted Richmond / Scott and Sandi Bergman.
p. cm.
ISBN-13: 978-1-59629-320-5 (alk. paper)
1. Ghosts--Virginia--Richmond. 2. Haunted places--Virginia--Richmond. I.
Bergman, Sandi. II. Title.
BF1472.U6B465 2007
133.09755'451--dc22
2007025192

CONTENTS

PREFACE

"What time does the ghost tour leave?"
"Where all does the tour take you?"
"Do you actually see any ghosts on the tour?"

These are the questions that are responsible for the creation of this book.

They sound like perfectly reasonable questions, except that at the time they were being asked, there was no ghost tour. We opened Haunts of Richmond in 2004. Scott has always been a ghost story and horror fan with a particular passion for walkthrough haunted attractions, commonly called "haunted houses." After years of research into the haunted attraction industry (yes, it is an industry), Scott persuaded Sandi that they should open their own haunted house. What would make Haunts of Richmond different from, say, "Dr. Tongue's House of Gore" was that instead of chasing people with chainsaws, all of the content would be based on local Richmond ghost stories, legends and dark history (to this point there have been no chainsaw murders in Richmond). We visited the London Dungeon dark attraction and saw how the Brits were celebrating their long, dark history. We figured that with Richmond's four hundred years of history and close association with Edgar Allan Poe, we had as good a chance of pulling off a year-round dark attraction in Virginia's capital city as any city in the country. After doing substantial research into local ghost stories, we leased a space on Eighteenth Street in historic Shockoe Bottom, developed a script, assembled a technical production team and hired actors to create a historically based attraction. Haunts of Richmond's "Widow's House" haunted attraction opened in October of 2004.

From the start, customers going through the Widow's House really enjoyed the fact that the scares and scenes were based in reality. However, it didn't take long for people to get confused by the historical and museum-like aspects of Haunts of Richmond. Thanks to successful ghost tours in cities like Key West, New Orleans, Charleston, Savannah and Gettysburg, just to name a few, when people think of haunted history, they think ghost tour.

It didn't take long before the number of questions about our assumed ghost tour started to indicate that we had an opportunity on our hands. Starting with the material we had already researched for the Widow's House, Sandi began to compile more information and to scout locations. In May of 2005, the Shadows of Shockoe Ghost Tour was launched, with Sandi as the first tour guide. Sandi found that as she gave tours, she would collect a number of new and different ghost stories from people on the tour, with many of the stories focusing on local sites. The tour grew and evolved until the Shadows of Shockoe Ghost Tour has become as important to Haunts of Richmond as the walkthrough attraction, which is now seasonal.

It seemed completely natural to us that we should capture many of the ghost stories on the Shadows of Shockoe Ghost Tour in a publication. And that is how *Haunted Richmond* came to be.

ACKNOWLEDGEMENTS

We wish to thank the many people who made this book possible. First and foremost, thanks to all of the staff members at Haunts of Richmond, whose boundless energy and enthusiasm has been an inspiration to us. Thanks to our families and friends for their support, especially our photographer and dear friend Jon Hood. Thanks to all those who helped us with our research, including the reference staffs of the Virginia Historical Society and Virginia State Library, and the good folks at the Poe Museum and Valentine Richmond History Center. Thanks to all those who have contributed information and stories, including the Virginia Capitol Police, patrons of the Shadows of Shockoe Ghost Tour and the many business owners and employees in Shockoe Bottom.

We also wish to acknowledge a debt of gratitude to L.B. Taylor and Marguerite Du Pont Lee for their classic local ghost story collections.

INTRODUCTION

Many haunted history and ghost story books are quite interesting, but there is something special about physically standing at or near the site where some great tragedy or trauma occurred and knowing that others have experienced paranormal activity in that spot. It is this connection that makes a ghost tour such a great activity. On the other hand, after the tour is over, it is easy to forget the stories and the history behind what was presented by the tour guide.

This book was born from the Shadows of Shockoe Ghost Tour at Haunts of Richmond in Richmond, Virginia. The intent is to present the haunted history contained herein in much the same way it would be delivered on a walking tour. We call it a virtual tour, and the stories are arranged in such a way that one could use this book for a self-guided tour of haunted sites in Richmond. The chapter order and contents are not identical to the Shadows of Shockoe Tour, but give a good approximation of what the tour is like.

With over four hundred years of history, Richmond has its share of ghostly and ghastly tales. Shockoe Bottom, Richmond's oldest neighborhood, has been at the epicenter of some of the most profound and tragic events in United States, Virginia and Richmond history. The area surrounding the Shockoe Valley has been the backdrop for the destruction of indigenous peoples, a revolution, the birth of a nation, foreign and domestic wars, famine, disease, floods, fires and engineering disasters, to name some of the causes of turmoil, tragedy and trauma experienced in the capital city. If a premature exit from this world is the primary reason for paranormal activity, then it is no wonder that there are so many shadows to be found in Shockoe.

Now put on your virtual walking shoes and grab a bottle of water as we assemble at the 17th Street Farmers' Market fronting on Main Street in downtown Richmond. Bring your camera, because you never know what you might catch on film or flash drive.

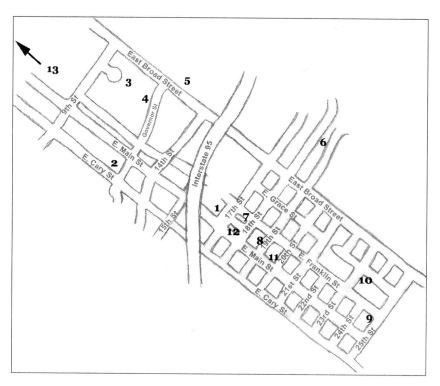

Map of stops mentioned in book. *Courtesy of Scott and Sandi Bergman.*

1

The Permanent Guests of the YMCA

O ur tour begins on Main Street in front of Richmond's historic 17th Street Farmers' Market. The market has been in operation since the late eighteenth century and has been a silent witness to Richmond's evolution, triumphs and tragedies since the founding of the United States. Our first stop is just a few yards from the market. As we face west and cross the southbound section of Seventeenth Street, we pass in front of a large brick building with a granite staircase that descends from the second-story patio and main entrance down to street level. Immediately to the left of the building is a parking lot, and to the left of that lot is a grand old train station. The lovely brick station designed in the French Renaissance style features a magnificent clock tower that climbs above the level of the raised interstate highway running through the Shockoe Valley.

Richmond's landmark passenger train depot, known as Main Street Station, opened in 1901 and supported passenger rail traffic until being decommissioned in 1971. Limited passenger service returned to the station in 2004. Around 1907, the Young Men's Christian Association had a building constructed at the corner of Main and Seventeenth Streets. The impressive five-story brick building, known as the Railroad YMCA Building, is a fine architectural match with the style of Main Street Station, and makes an attractive neighbor to the rail station. Given the YMCA's mission of providing a safe haven and healthy activities to those in need, the proximity of the new building to Main Street Station made it an ideal location for the charity organization to conduct its business. Many people coming to Richmond to find employment came by train, and the prominent YMCA building was bound to catch the attention of the new arrivals. The Railroad YMCA operated in the 1500 block of Main Street until the 1960s, when services from the central

The Railroad YMCA, built in 1907. *Courtesy of Virginia State Library.*

YMCA at Sixth and Main Streets and other locations around town were deemed sufficient to carry out the organization's mission.

Currently, the Railroad YMCA Building houses two restaurants on the lower floors and residential apartments on the upper floors. One of the restaurants is situated in the front of the building opening onto Main Street. The other restaurant, which is an Irish pub, sits in the rear of the building, facing the Farmers' Market. The owners of the pub have put their hearts and souls into the establishment, and neither acts of nature nor supernatural phenomena have been able to deter them from living out their dream.

In September of 2004, a gentleman named Tommy signed the papers authorizing him to take over the commercial space at the rear of 1548 East Main Street. It should have been a day of celebration, but it quickly turned into a day of misery. On the very day that Tommy signed the lease, Tropical Storm Gaston stalled over Richmond and dumped thirteen inches of rain in only eight hours. The tremendous amount of rain in such a short period of time caused massive flooding across the city and surrounding counties. Some of the worst damage was done in the flood-prone streets of Shockoe Bottom.

At one time, a tributary of the James River known as Shockoe Creek meandered down the Shockoe Valley, flowing through Shockoe Bottom on its way. The low-lying bottom has always been vulnerable to flooding with tragic loss of human life, livestock and property. In the 1920s, Shockoe Creek was walled in to prevent it from contributing to the flooding problems in the city. Today, there is very little evidence of the existence of the creek. Historically, most of the flooding problems have occurred when the James River tops its banks, so the city built a floodwall to protect the low-lying areas. In 2004, the floodwall gave Richmonders a false sense of security about the flood risk in Shockoe Bottom. With the arrival of Gaston, an old wound was opened. The floodwaters did not come from the river, but from excessive rainwater running down off the surrounding hills along the old Shockoe Creek path. The floodwaters rushing through the Farmers' Market rose eight feet in half an hour, catching people off guard. Cars were washed away and most of the buildings from South Fourteenth to the corner of Seventeenth and East Franklin Streets were flooded—some all the way to the second floor. A delivery truck floated down Seventeenth street, crashing into a building with so much force that it knocked the entire building down. Cars floated to the level of the Farmers' Market roof. The amount of rain brought by Gaston was extraordinary, called by meteorologists a "once-in-three-thousand-year event."

Tommy's new pub was completely flooded, leaving a muddy mess as the water receded. The whole restaurant had to be renovated. Tommy and his family worked tirelessly to get the devastated restaurant in condition to open in 2005. Tommy, his wife and their daughters all put in time working in the pub.

One afternoon, the family was in the restaurant preparing for the opening. The oldest daughter came out of the kitchen looking a bit shaky. She told the family that she had just seen a strange man in the kitchen. The young lady was working and happened to glance up to see a man standing against the wall, just watching her. She looked away, not really registering what she had just seen. Then, as it hit her, she looked up again, but he was gone. The family was skeptical of the daughter's claim. It took a few weeks and another sighting for the family to actually believe her. One night, Tommy's youngest daughter also had a close encounter with the spirit in the kitchen. She was closing up and was back in the kitchen alone washing some dishes. The young lady had plans to meet up with a friend later that night, but since he too was working in a local restaurant, she didn't expect him to arrive until fairly late in the evening. As she stood over the sink, the young woman sensed someone walk up behind her. Assuming it was her friend, she turned around, ready to give the young man a piece of her mind for not announcing himself. As she turned, she saw that it wasn't her friend standing behind her. It was a man she didn't recognize, watching over her shoulder. The startled woman immediately flinched, as she stood rooted to her spot. As she flinched, the man vanished completely.

Rosie Connolly's pub, where there is plenty of "help" in the kitchen. *Photo by Jon Hood.*

In short order, she did too, fleeing the scene of the manifestation! Family and staff still get the feeling of being watched by invisible eyes in various parts of the restaurant, typically back in the kitchen and near the restrooms.

On one occasion, a patron stopped one of the servers and told her that while he was inside the restroom with the door locked, a man walked right through the room without opening the door. The server didn't say how many spirits the patron had consumed before telling her about the spirit walking through the restroom door.

One evening, while the authors were sitting out on the patio at the pub enjoying a pint, Tommy came out and relayed a new story. One of his newer servers had heard about the haunting of the kitchen and wanted very much to see the ghost. One afternoon the server found herself alone in the kitchen, and she noticed a young lady standing in the salad preparation area. The mysterious young lady was dressed as though she was going to a party, wearing a long satin dress, her hair up in a bun and a long pearl necklace around her neck. As the server looked on, the woman didn't move, but just stood there as if admiring herself in a mirror. Then it dawned on the server that she was probably looking at a ghost. Recalling that the other ghost seemed to disappear when someone looked away and then looked back, the server tried the old spirit dismissal trick. The trick failed. When the server looked again, the opulently dressed woman was still there. Confused, the server promptly went to the dining room to get one of the family members to take a look. However, when the server and the family member entered the kitchen, there was no trace of the woman in the satin dress. This is the only occasion to date that the female spirit has been seen.

Interestingly, no one on the staff has had the feelings of being watched or witnessed anything ghostly at all in the dining room or the bar, both of which are located in an addition to the building. Perhaps it is because these areas were outside of the building when the ghosts who inhabit it were living there. The male ghost has only been seen for an instant, not even long enough for anyone to tell us what kind of clothing he is wearing. The female ghost was seen only once by one person. We have been able to find very little in the way of historical details of the Railroad YMCA that might help explain the identity of the reported ghosts. Perhaps they are people who once took shelter at the YMCA and when they died, their spirits returned to a place where they felt safe and comfortable. The YMCA strives to build healthy spirits, minds and bodies. In the case of the Railroad YMCA, it seems that they successfully fulfilled their mission in the spirit department!

2.

LADIES AND LOCKS

Our tour now heads west on Main Street toward Fourteenth Street. As we walk along, bear in mind that portions of the open parking areas we are passing were once home to slave trading facilities. In fact, just behind Main Street Station is the site of Lumpkin's Slave Prison, which earned the nickname of the "Devil's Half Acre" due to the abysmal conditions that thousands of African Americans were forced to endure there. At Fourteenth Street, we turn left and go one block to Cary Street, where we turn right. We head up the hill along the cobblestone street into historic Shockoe Slip.

The area surrounding the turning basin on the Kanawha canal was the heart of trade in the thriving city of Richmond in the mid-nineteenth century. The area, which runs uphill moving west from Shockoe Bottom, is known as Shockoe Slip, and it was home to many of the businesses that supported the busy shipping industry along the James River. Flourmills, tobacco warehouses, produce and dry goods stores, apparel and hat factories, public taverns and inns could all be found within the boundaries of the city. Tragically, most of these buildings were destroyed in the evacuation fire at the close of the Civil War in 1865. The area was quickly rebuilt in the decade following the war, and many of the postwar generation buildings still stand today. Shockoe Slip is now an area rich in culture, cuisine and shopping. The historic buildings and cobblestones of Cary Street Road exude an old-fashioned ambience and charm that provide a unique glimpse into Richmond's past.

Over the years, Shockoe Slip has seen its share of excitement. Given easy access to rushing river water, Shockoe Slip was home to most of the flourmills that operated in Richmond. Flour that was milled in Richmond was known for its smooth texture and resistance to humidity. By the 1860s, Richmond newspapers reported that Richmond was the largest distributor of flour in the world. The largest of the mills in Richmond was the Gallego Mill, which sat at the east end of the large canal turning basin. The Gallego Mill was destroyed by fire and rebuilt on several occasions over the ninety-five years of its productive life. The mill buildings were a staple of the landscape around the canal. But mills were not the only industry necessary to support shipping in the city. The sailors and merchants who frequented the city needed food and entertainment.

The building that stands at 1214 East Cary Street was completed in 1868, just a few years after the infamous conflagration at the end of the Civil War. Over the years this building has been put to several uses, serving as a tobacco warehouse, granary and more. As with many of the buildings in the Shockoe Slip and Shockoe Bottom neighborhoods, the last half of the twentieth century saw the building most often used as a restaurant and nightclub. Until 2010, it was home to a local brewery and restaurant and made a popular place to meet for dinner and cocktails. Rumor has it that during the early part of the 1800s the site where the brewery stands was the location of a brothel. Many of the spirits experienced in the building are believed to be the ladies who plied their trade here so many years ago.

The ghosts in this building are most often seen on the upper floors. Guests leaving the billiards room will pass the upstairs barroom on their way to the staircase. In the upper barroom, some folks occasionally catch a glimpse of one or more women clad in gauzy dresses walking in the club area. These mysterious ladies are sometimes spotted by people in the same room with them, often being mistaken for fellow patrons lingering at a table late in the evening. A second look at the table shows it empty only seconds after someone was seen sitting there.

These "women of the night" are experienced in the art of getting someone's attention. Managers and wait staff have reported hearing someone call their name, only to turn and find themselves alone in the room. Although the staff doesn't often see the women on the lower floor of the building, they are frequently heard moving about. One of the managers reported that when he was readying the restaurant to open for dinner one night, he heard footsteps walking across the wooden dining room floor. He could clearly see that there was no one in the room with him, but he heard the steps all the way across the room, even passing within a few feet of where he was standing. As the sound of the steps moved to the far side of the room, the manager distinctly heard someone call his name from the far corner of the dining room. On one occasion,

The buildings here were completed in the late 1860s after the evacuation fire had destroyed the buildings previously on this site. *Photo by Jon Hood.*

a gentleman whose job for the evening was to monitor the front door headed out to the foyer to open the establishment and begin greeting customers. The doorman was about ten feet from his post when he heard someone walk up behind him and whisper his name in his ear. When the doorman turned around there was nobody there.

The spectral ladies who inhabit the brewery are also quite mischievous when it comes to security. There is a room on the third floor that is used for storage of restaurant supplies and the ingredients for brewing beer. Because the brewmaster doesn't need any assistance from helpful customers, this room is secured each evening. There are two doors to the storeroom. The inner door has two padlocks, for which the manager has the keys. The outer door has a timed security lock on it. One night, as usual, the manager started working his way through the closing process. He started upstairs and was ready to lock up the storeroom, but he could only find one of the two padlocks. The padlocks are kept hanging on the door when not in use and are rarely moved. The manager searched the room and enlisted the help of some of the other staff, but to no avail. The manager went home that night with only one lock on the inner door, the outer door secured and the timer engaged. The next day the manager returned and made his way to the storeroom to open it for the day. He checked the timer on the security lock, and it had not been opened since he set it the previous night. When the manager opened the outer door, his eyes bulged at the sight of both padlocks on the inner door in their usual place and locked! He opened the inner door and took a quick inventory to confirm that nothing in the room had been taken or even moved around. It seemed that the ladies were having some fun at the manager's expense.

Just after the manager discovered both locks in place, one of the bartenders called upstairs on the intercom. The bartender reported that he had found the missing lock downstairs, behind the bar. When the bartender brought the newly discovered lock upstairs, the manager explained that the missing lock had "reappeared," and in fact, the lock that the bartender held was a different make altogether. Later that day, one of the kitchen staff reported that he too had found a lock on a shelf in the kitchen. Over the next few weeks the staff kept finding locks they didn't even know they had, all throughout the restaurant. Apparently, the ladies had decided to form their own lost and found department!

3.

RICHMOND'S HAUNTED CAPITOL

As we leave Shockoe Slip behind and head north up the imposing hill on Ninth Street, the magnificent and newly renovated Virginia State Capitol Building comes into view up the hill on our right. Thomas Jefferson's "temple of freedom" is lit up like a beacon atop the hill. We make our way into the serene, park-like setting of Capitol Square. Virginia's Capitol Building in Richmond is the second oldest continuously used statehouse in the United States, behind the statehouse in Annapolis, Maryland. The peaceful, secure feeling one gets when walking in the quiet of Capitol Square belies the exciting history of the building.

When the capital was moved to Richmond from Williamsburg in 1780, Thomas Jefferson was asked to design a suitable building. Construction on the Virginia Capitol began in 1785, and the building was put into service in 1788. Over the years, Mr. Jefferson's building has been altered and expanded to meet the legislative and judicial needs of a growing commonwealth. Many famous Americans have walked the venerable halls of Virginia's Capitol, including Patrick Henry, Thomas Jefferson, George Washington, James Monroe, Henry "Light-Horse Harry" Lee, William "Extra Billy" Smith and John Marshall. Sculptures and paintings of many renowned Virginia statesmen, politicians, judges and lawmakers reside in galleries throughout the building.

From the time it opened, the capitol was not only the meeting place for the Senate and Congress, but also home to the other two branches of state government. It was the scene of the much-heralded trial of Aaron Burr on charges of treason in 1807. On February 13, 1861, the State Secession Convention was launched at the capitol, resulting in Virginia's Ordinance of Secession published on April 17 of the same year. During the Civil War, the Confederate Congress met in the capitol until forced

The capitol after its 2007 face-lift. *Photo by Jon Hood.*

Interior room with portraits of famous Virginians. *Courtesy of Virginia State Library.*

to flee the city in 1865. The Supreme Court of Virginia used a chamber on the second story of the building as its courtroom for many years. This second-story courtroom was the setting for the most horrific event in the capitol's history—an event that would doom many unfortunate souls to centuries of unrest. After making our way up Capitol Hill, we stop under some trees on the lawn in front of the commanding structure before us. A breeze blows gently through the branches as we recall the sociopolitical backdrop to the tragic scene that unfolded here in April of 1870.

Virginia came under federal military rule immediately after the Confederate government left the city in 1865. Reconstruction was a time of tremendous change for both the state of Virginia and the city of Richmond as each struggled to regain control of its own affairs, recover from the physical, economic and social devastation of the war and come to terms with emancipation and the changing role of African Americans in society. The leaders during this time were military governors, appointed by the federal government, not elected by popular vote. By January of 1870, the federal hand had withdrawn, and once again Richmond was in control of its own political destiny. The general assembly gave permission to the city council to appoint a new mayor for the city of Richmond. The man they appointed was Henry K. Ellyson. Ellyson was a Southerner and a conservative who had strong political backing in parts of the city, including many former Confederate veterans. However, the man who had been serving as mayor, the Northerner George Chahoon, also had strong political backing, along with control of the local police force, and he refused to yield power to what he considered an illegitimate successor. For a time, both men were acting as mayor simultaneously, which ultimately led to an armed confrontation and bloodshed on both sides. The tense mayoral situation lasted for several months as attempts were made to find a peaceful resolution. During that time, the case made its way through the judicial system and came to rest in the hands of the Virginia State Supreme Court of Appeals.

On April 27, 1870, the greatly anticipated hearing took place in the courtroom at the capitol. The conflict had been widely reported in the newspapers, and the importance of the forthcoming landmark decision was not lost on the citizens of Richmond. Hundreds of people turned out on Capitol Hill to attend the trial. The second-story courtroom was packed with the early birds who were able to find space inside. As the available seating in the courtroom dwindled, spectators ascended the stairs to the gallery above. Moments before the proceedings began,

Virginia's State Capitol Building in the 1890s. *Courtesy of the Valentine Museum.*

both the courtroom and gallery were crammed full of people eagerly awaiting the decision on Richmond's political fate.

According to *Harper's Weekly Journal of Civilization*, the bells had just tolled eleven o'clock. One of the judges and the clerk of the court had just entered the courtroom when suddenly there was a loud cracking sound as a primary girder in the courtroom floor snapped in half, causing the entire surface of the floor to severely bow in the center. The movement of the floor then destabilized the beams supporting the gallery, which was pulled away from the wall and crashed, along with its human occupants, into the center of the crowded courtroom floor. The force from the collapse of the gallery and the weight of its human burden were too much for the courtroom floor to withstand. *Harper's* reported that the floor "was crushed through as if it had been glass." Wood, plaster, iron, flesh and bone fell through to the House of Delegates chamber below, those in the gallery having fallen some forty feet in all. A cloud of dust rose from the devastated building like smoke from a fire.

Rescuers descended upon the building only to find a ruined shell containing a mass of dead and wounded entangled in the wreckage. Hundreds of people were injured, crushed by the falling infrastructure or suffocated by dust. In describing the sounds issuing forth from the accident scene, *Harper's* used the haunting phrase, "cries and groans arose that none who heard will ever forget." Firemen, citizens and uninjured spectators joined in the effort of pulling the dead and wounded out of the building and placing them under the trees in the square to await identification and/or medical attention. The victims were so thoroughly covered in plaster dust and blood that many were unrecognizable until they could be cleaned up. A reporter who had been killed in the collapse was so badly disfigured that his own wife did not recognize him. It wasn't until his pockets were searched that he was identified. As we stand on the very same ground where the triage of the victims took place, we imagine the billowing dust cloud issuing forth from the ruined building and the shock, panic and chaos that rocked Richmond on that spring day in 1870.

The casualty list shocked Richmond: sixty-two men dead and over two hundred injured. Among the dead were several prominent citizens and lawmakers. Both of the contending mayoral candidates survived the collapse with only minor injuries. Had the House of Delegates, whose chamber was below the courtroom, been in session, the tragedy would have been even worse.

While conducting the Shadows of Shockoe Ghost Tour, we have had an opportunity to collect a number of first- and secondhand ghost stories related to us from members of the highly esteemed Virginia Capitol Police. Let us take a moment to say that the members of the Capitol Police with whom we interact have been highly professional, courteous and extremely helpful in making the Shadows of Shockoe tour a success. This is commendable in our security-conscious post–9/11 world, given that our tour stops by the grounds late at night with flashbulbs flashing and ghost stories flying about the capitol and the Executive Mansion.

The Virginia Capitol Police Department is the oldest police force in the United States, having been commissioned in 1618 when the capital was still located in Jamestown. Of course, the department itself does not officially recognize the existence of ghosts on the capitol grounds, but we have been told some hair-raising stories from the people who spend the most time in and around the capitol at night and on holidays when the buildings are mostly empty.

Some officers who work in the building at night, when things are very quiet, say that they occasionally hear muffled shrieks and moans echo through the halls. It seems that the sounds mainly emanate from the area of the basement below the room where the delegates chamber used to reside until extensive renovations at the turn of the twentieth century. Are these the sounds of the victims of the capitol collapse, still seeking a

Rendering of the catastrophe at the capitol. *Courtesy of Virginia State Library.*

way out of the horrible mound of wreckage where they lost their lives? When recalling *Harper's* chilling description of the moans and groans in the aftermath of the collapse, it is easy to believe that these terrible sounds would be the paranormal manifestations of the tragedy repeated over and over again throughout the years.

The high ceilings and plaster walls of the capitol building give rise to some strange acoustics and echoes. People hear the sound of footsteps on floors above and in the next room when nobody is believed to be in those rooms. In the middle of the night, conversations can be heard, but are just a bit too quiet or distorted to be understood. Over time, the folks working the graveyard shift at the capitol building start to get used to the sight of doors that were closed a few minutes ago now standing open. Events such as water fountains that run for seemingly no reason, and lights that turn on and off by themselves, become regular occurrences. However, a couple of stories describe events beyond the usual ghostly occurrences in Capitol Square.

An officer performing a routine security sweep of the building one night passed a gentleman moving in the opposite direction down a hallway. The two men exchanged salutations in passing. The gentleman did not seem out of place, so the officer did not immediately question his presence. After taking a few steps, however, the officer realized he had not seen the requisite identification badge on the man and turned around to ask the gentleman to show his badge. The man continued to walk away in a casual manner as if he didn't hear the officer call to him. The officer followed down the hall trying to get the attention of the gentleman. At the end of the hall, the gentleman turned a corner, with the officer about five steps behind him. When the officer turned the corner, the man was nowhere in sight. The officer radioed back to the control room that there was an intruder in the building. The building was locked down and several additional officers were sent in to find the mysterious gentleman. An exhaustive search was performed and the officers concluded that the man was no longer in the building. Later that night, while the search team was debriefing in one of the upstairs rooms, the officer who had seen the gentleman happened to glance up at the portraits on the wall. He suddenly realized that he was looking at a portrait of the very person they were searching for. And just as suddenly, he realized they weren't going to find him, because the man in the portrait had died years earlier!

Being the seat of the Confederate government during the Civil War, Capitol Square saw a great deal of activity from 1861 to 1865. However, Confederate military forces abandoned and set fire to Richmond before the Union army entered the city. We are not aware of any actual combat ever taking place in the area immediately surrounding the capitol. This makes the next story even more perplexing. The Capitol Square grounds are closed to the public each night at 11:00 p.m. One night well after 11:00 p.m., the officer on duty in the guardhouse on the western side of the complex sent out a call on the radio that he had just sighted a group of uniformed Civil War re-enactors making their way across the lawn toward the Executive Mansion, and since the grounds were closed and the Capitol Police were not informed of any approved special event, the group should be escorted off the grounds. Officers at the other guardhouse in front of the Executive Mansion went out to intercept the wayward re-enactors, but much to their surprise, they never saw the group marching toward them. The officers looked all over the grounds, but the phantom company was never found. The officer who originally spotted the group insisted that he had seen at least twenty men dressed in what appeared to be Confederate uniforms, marching across the lawn. He was at a loss to explain how his eyes could have played such a trick on him or how such a large group could have eluded the search party and made their way off the grounds without being seen by anyone else.

We now leave the stately capitol building with the distinct feeling that the Capitol Police and our tour group are not the only ones on the grounds. We make our way east across the square to Virginia's Executive Mansion.

4.

THE GHOST OF
THE GOVERNOR'S MANSION

As we make our way east across Richmond's Capitol Square, we approach Virginia's Executive Mansion. This grand building, which is the oldest continuously occupied state governor's residence in the United States, was completed in 1813. The first family to inhabit the mansion was that of Governor James Barbour. Sadly, the previous governor, George William Smith, who would have been the first governor to live in the house, died tragically in the great theatre fire of 1811.

The Executive Mansion is a center of hospitality for the state, where Virginia's first family receives many distinguished guests. Guests have included several presidents of the United States, foreign dignitaries and sports and entertainment figures. In May of 2007, Queen Elizabeth II of Great Britain visited the Executive Mansion as part of her tour in honor of the four hundredth anniversary of the settlement of Jamestown. The bodies of such disparate figures as Confederate General Thomas "Stonewall" Jackson and tennis player and humanitarian Arthur Ashe have lain in state in the Executive Mansion.

Like the capitol building, there are many stories of unexplained occurrences and paranormal activity in the Executive Mansion. Keep an eye on the second-story windows as we relay some of these stories. You might just see a face looking back at you.

The most famous permanent resident of the Executive Mansion is the so-called "Gray Lady." Although her identity is unknown, the specter seen in the mansion is reported to be that of a young woman. Legend has it that on a cold winter's evening some time in the mid-1800s, a young lady attended a party hosted at the Executive Mansion. Due to the icy conditions, the governor insisted that the young woman stay at the mansion overnight to allow the weather to clear. The next morning, the

Front hallway of the Executive Mansion. *Courtesy of Virginia State Library.*

young lady, still wearing her blue taffeta gown, boarded a carriage and departed for home. On the way down the steep slope of the road leaving Capitol Hill, the carriage overturned, and the young lady was thrown to her death. Some people reason that the young woman returned to the last place on earth where she was happy.

According to L.B. Taylor in his book *The Ghosts of Richmond and Nearby Environs*, the first known sighting of the phantom dates all the way back to the 1890s, when Governor Philip McKinney had a run-in with her. As Taylor tells the story, one summer afternoon, Governor McKinney retired to the second story of the mansion and stopped by a bathroom to freshen up. As McKinney stepped from the bathroom into an adjoining bedroom, he spied a young woman whom he did not recognize sitting in front of a window. Embarrassed, the governor excused himself and immediately headed for the first lady's chambers. The flustered governor asked his wife who the guest was in the bedroom. The first lady replied that she had no guest and together the couple entered the room to get to the bottom of the matter. The woman was gone.

Since Governor McKinney's experience, other governors and their families, staff members and security officers have seen the Gray Lady. On two separate occasions a butler and the brother of one of the governors have supposedly chased the Gray Lady through the mansion only to watch her disappear in the basement and out the front door, respectively. A Capitol Police officer once saw the woman upstairs on the floor reserved for the governor's family. Mistaking her for an unauthorized visitor of the mortal variety, the officer approached the young woman to tell her that the area was restricted. As the officer approached, the woman suddenly vanished, leaving just a stir of the curtains. Many people have reported hearing footsteps and the swooshing sound of the young woman's taffeta gown as she moves about the mansion. On one hot summer's day, an officer felt a cold spot in the basement and, much to his amazement, one of the windows frosted over temporarily. Yet another officer quit on the spot when he was on duty in the basement one evening and felt an invisible hand touch his face.

As with the stories of the capitol building, the tour guides on the Shadows of Shockoe Ghost Tour have been able to pick up quite a few creepy tales from the Capitol Police officers on duty at the Executive Mansion. Apparently, one doesn't work there long before experiencing something that indicates that the Gray Lady is still around. Similar to incidents reported from other sources, doors closing when there is no

The Executive Mansion in Richmond, Virginia. *Photo by Jon Hood.*

one upstairs in the house, the sound of footsteps in the basement and the swish of a taffeta skirt are common occurrences.

Occasionally things have gone missing, only to turn up later in improbable places. An example of this is a recent governor who "misplaced" a favorite pair of shoes. The family and staff looked for them for weeks, but the shoes apparently had walked off. About six months after the shoes went missing, they reappeared just as mysteriously as they had vanished. One morning, a staff member whose office was in the basement arrived at work only to find the shoes sitting on his desk!

An officer recently told one of the Shadows of Shockoe tour guides that one morning while he was walking up the main staircase to leave the newspaper for the governor, something caught his attention. The officer couldn't say whether it was a movement or a noise, but for some reason he turned and looked at the wall a few steps below the stair where he stood. There was a mirror on the wall and in that mirror he saw the reflection of a young woman standing behind him. Upon turning the rest of the way around, the startled officer saw that there was no one on the stairs with him. One day, an officer saw the woman peering out of a second-floor window at a time when nobody was supposed to be in the mansion, and certainly not in the governor's quarters. The officer ran inside to confront the intruder, but after a thorough search, he had to admit there was no one upstairs.

One officer, who has experienced the presence of the Gray Lady many times, related an experience with another ghost in the mansion. The officer was monitoring some security equipment in a restricted area on the first floor of the mansion. He heard footsteps behind him, and when he turned around he saw a tall, slim, African American gentleman dressed in a tuxedo and wearing white gloves, carrying a full silver tea service. The gentleman turned and walked into the next room, followed by the officer. When the officer entered the room, the gentleman was nowhere to be seen. The officer said that he radioed to the control room to alert them, but he knew from the start that they would not find anyone. In the officer's opinion, the gentleman was a butler who had worked there years ago when the serving staff wore formal uniforms of that sort. Apparently, the butler was still attending to his duties and serving afternoon tea.

Mark Holmberg, in a *Richmond Times-Dispatch* article, quoted former Governor Linwood Holton as saying that he and his family "saw the evidence (of her presence) on three occasions." Holton reported that during Hurricane Agnes in 1972, power to Capitol Square was lost for an extended period of time, but a light in the "ladies staircase" remained on. None of the governor's staff was able to figure out how the light stayed on when all the power was out. One time while the governor and his family were away, a saltshaker was emptied all over a table, despite the room being under guard. The third incident occurred one night when Governor Holton was awakened from his sleep by the sound of a number of large portraits being pushed over onto the rug in the bedroom with him. Holton did not see the ghost, but took her prank in stride, saying that he believed she did it to "tease me a little bit." Governor Holton's daughter, Anne, married Timothy Kaine, who became governor in 2006. Virginia's first lady is now enjoying her second stay in the lovely residence, with all the history, charm and spirits that come with it.

The Gray Lady seems to be fond of children. Members of the governor's staff recently told our guides two stories in which the permanent resident of the mansion revealed herself to youngsters. In the first incident, the first lady's three-year-old nephew was visiting the Executive Mansion. His mother was holding him such that he was looking over her shoulder at the staircase leading to the second story. Out of the blue, the child asked his mother who the lady on the stairs smiling at him was. When his mother turned to look, there was no one on the stairs. The second occurrence involves the son of a longtime member of the mansion housekeeping staff. At the time of the incident, the boy was around ten years old. One Saturday when the governor and his family were out of town, the housekeeper needed to visit the mansion briefly on an errand. She had her son with her and quickly completed the task inside the house. As the mother was driving the pair away from the house, her son exclaimed that he saw a woman waving to him from an upstairs window in the mansion. The skeptical housekeeper reminded the boy that the governor's family was away, and therefore there was no one in the house, but the boy insisted that he saw a woman and described her clearly enough that the mother's curiosity was piqued. However, after turning around and carefully inspecting the windows of the mansion, the housekeeper saw no sign of anyone looking out.

In a newspaper article, Roxane Gilmore, wife of former Governor James Gilmore, described two frightening events that occurred when she, James and their two sons lived in the Executive Mansion in the late 1990s. In one incident, one of the boy's bedspreads was found lying in the hall outside of his bedroom. In another incident, the other boy's bed was moved halfway across the bedroom by some unseen force.

Ghost stories connected with the Executive Mansion are so well known that each governor is inevitably asked about any supernatural phenomena experienced while living in the mansion. That is certainly an unusual requirement for Virginia's top executive—supernatural spin control! As recently as December of 2006, Governor Timothy Kaine told listeners on a radio program that he is the recipient of some persistent and unexplained phone calls. It seems that the phone in the private quarters of the mansion will ring at a "very inconvenient time." When the governor picks up the phone, there is no one on the line. The calls come in regularly at the same time on the same night of the week. The director of the Executive Mansion told the *Virginian-Pilot* newspaper that former Governor Mark Warner received the same creepy calls. Perhaps it is the ghost of a former Republican governor playing a prank on the Democrats from the other side!

5.

MONUMENTAL CHURCH

Imagine the deep mournful wail of a heavy iron cemetery gate as it slowly swings open. This gives you some idea of the sensation that one feels walking through the church gate at Richmond's Monumental Church on Broad Street just across from Capitol Square. The creepy sound of the gate alone has sent some of the guests on the Shadows of Shockoe Ghost Tour scurrying. If we are fortunate enough to find the gate unlocked, we will make our way through the yard and up the steps to the classical portico of the church. In a vault beneath the portico on which we stand lie the remains of seventy-two people who lost their lives in the great theatre fire of 1811. Our footsteps gently echo through the colonnade, as some members of the group gather around the sculpted urn in the center of the portico, and some stop to read the names of the dead on a bronze plaque on the front wall of the church. Silence descends upon the group as the true significance of this place sinks in.

Richmond in the early 1800s was an important city politically, economically and culturally. The city was growing rapidly. Shockoe Hill, which had recently been renamed Capitol Hill, was quickly becoming the center of social activity with the seat of government, the teaching hospital, various churches, houses and a theatre located on its heights. The Old Richmond Theatre stood on the north side of Broad Street between what is now Twelfth and College Streets. Many important actors of the day performed in the theatre, including Elizabeth Poe, who brought her young son Edgar to Richmond with her in 1810. Elizabeth Poe died of consumption in early December of 1811, just weeks before the theatre would burn to the ground.

Richmonders were enjoying the holiday season. A special theatre performance slated for December 23 had been rescheduled due to bad

Terrified crowd fleeing the flames as the theatre burns to the ground. *Courtesy of Virginia State Library.*

weather, and the whole city looked forward to the event. The performance occurred on December 26, 1811. More than six hundred people attended, which constituted about 6 percent of the total population of the city. The event was so popular that even the governor of Virginia, George W. Smith, was in attendance. Men and women in their holiday finery filed in to the theatre through the narrow doorways to find seats in the orchestra or upstairs in one of the balconies. After the main production was complete, an after-show pantomime called *Raymond and Agnes or The Bleeding Nun* began. The first act was well received and after a musical interlude, action in the second act began.

Behind the stage curtain, stagehands were moving scenery into place for the remainder of the show. A chandelier holding a lighted oil lamp was hanging in the wrong place and a stagehand was ordered to move it quickly. The young stagehand looked up and saw that raising the chandelier would bring it close to backdrops hanging in the fly gallery. The stagehand protested, but the stage manager told him in no uncertain terms to get the chandelier out of the way. The stagehand obeyed and, as feared, the lamp in the chandelier came into contact with the backdrop, setting it on fire. The stagehand immediately called to another worker to cut down the backdrop, but when that young man saw the fire, he panicked and ran from the theatre. The flames quickly reached the ceiling, and the fire began to spread out of control. The fire was hidden from the audience by the stage curtain. In fact, when small burning pieces of the ceiling began to fall on to the stage, most of the patrons thought it was part of the production. When one of the actors came to the front of the stage and uttered the immortal phrase "The house is on fire," bedlam erupted.

The audience panicked and attempted to flee. Six hundred people all headed for the exits simultaneously. Those backstage and in the orchestra pit used a little-known side door and quickly got out. Many in the upper balcony had a clear exit as well, but those in the main seating and in the first balcony jammed the narrow primary exits. Pitiful cries and screams rose up as victims pleaded to be rescued. The house quickly filled with deadly smoke, suffocating those caught in the crush. One man reported that he and his wife were making their way to the door when she remembered that she had left something in her seat. Before he could stop her, she went back to retrieve the forgotten item, not fully understanding the urgency of the situation. The man's wife never made it out. Ladies running for the stairs in their full skirts tripped and fell, only to be trampled. Many audience members tried to jump to safety from the second-story windows, sustaining a spectrum of injuries.

News of the fire spread quickly and residents living near the theatre rushed to assist. As they approached, the residents saw a scene of horror, with people screaming and crying as they tried to find loved ones in the confused and terrified crowd. Closer to the theatre, the scene got worse. From the ground, people could be seen through second-floor windows being consumed by flames with no means of escape.

There were heroes whose bravery distinguished them on that terrible night. James McCaw, a well-known doctor from the teaching hospital just up the hill, found himself trapped on the second floor. McCaw broke out a window and looked for assistance on the ground. He caught sight of Gilbert Hunt, a blacksmith who had been alerted to the fire when the alarm bells rang. The blacksmith saw the doctor in the window and agreed to work with him. Dr. McCaw began to guide people out the window with Mr. Hunt below to break their fall. Together the two men saved a dozen people. When there was no one else to assist, McCaw jumped from the window, only to be caught on a piece of iron that protruded from the outer wall. Gilbert Hunt was able to pull Dr. McCaw to safety just as the outer wall began to crumble.

Governor Smith got out of the theater safely, but plunged back in to find his missing child and never emerged a second time. Several other rescuers pushed their luck and met the same fate as the governor.

Within ten minutes of the start of the fire, the entire building was in flames. Rescue attempts were curtailed when the walls began to fall. The building burned to the ground, and many of the victims were not located until their remains were sifted from the ashes. As the days passed, the death toll continued to climb as more victims were identified and some of those who survived that fateful night succumbed to their injuries. The final death toll was recorded as seventy-two.

Many of the bodies found in the ashes were so badly burned that they could not be identified. The decision was made to gather all of the remains together to be buried in two mahogany boxes in the cemetery at St. John's Church. However, many of the bones turned to dust and could not be collected, so the ground where the theatre stood was consecrated and the boxes were buried on the site of the tragedy. To honor those who died, Monumental Church, which stands before our tour group, was built on the consecrated ground and was dedicated in 1814. Over the years, two stories of fateful premonitions involving the theatre fire have surfaced.

One of the stories that came out of the tragedy is that of two young lovers, Sallie Conyers and Lieutenant James Gibbon. The story was published in a *Richmond Times-Dispatch* article in 1937. Our thanks to the

Gilbert Hunt, who heroically saved more than a dozen people from the flames. *Courtesy of Virginia State Library.*

Sallie Conyers, who died in the arms of her love, James Gibbon. *Courtesy of RichmondNowandThen.com.*

"Richmond Then and Now" website for posting the contents of the article. Conyers and Gibbon were involved in a whirlwind romance late in 1811 and by December, they were engaged to be married. James, who was a naval officer, received notice to report to his ship just after the holidays in 1811. As the couple was so young, Sallie's mother determined that they should wait to get married until James had returned from the sea. The young couple planned to attend the theatre performance at the Old Richmond Theatre on December 26 with a group of friends.

On Christmas night, James Gibbon dreamed that he was standing in front of a closed door. Some unknown horror behind the door made him fearful of passing through it. Then the door opened and he found himself in a large dark hall. In the dream, James saw a man's face illuminated by a "lurid light" and the man's eyes were fixed upon him. The dream depressed James Gibbon so much that he stayed in from the festivities

Monumental Church, dedicated in 1814. *Photo by Jon Hood.*

during the next day and considered not attending the theatre that night. Ultimately, both Sallie and James went to the theatre that evening and sat with their own families. During the first act of the pantomime, James was horrified when he recognized the face of an actor onstage as that of the man in his nightmare. Upset, James left the theatre after the first act and went to Capitol Square to await Sallie. When the alarm bells sounded, Gibbon rushed back to the theatre and ran inside to find his love. Although James Gibbon did find Sallie Conyers in the burning theatre, the young lovers were unable to make it back out of the building, and perished in each other's arms. Their remains were identified together in the ruins, James by the buttons from his uniform and Sallie by the necklace that James's sister had helped her choose for the evening.

It seems that another audience member received a warning not to attend the theatre on that fateful December evening. In an intriguing manuscript housed in the Virginia Historical Society, Mrs. Nannie Dunlop Werth recorded a story passed down to her from her grandmother, a Mrs. McRae. Written in 1922, the piece is entitled "A True Ghost Story." The story is that of a young lady named Nancy Green who had been adopted into the family of Patrick Gibson. Nancy's birthday was on December 27, and she was about to turn sixteen years old. Nancy's father, J.W. Green, was an actor and was scheduled to perform in the pantomime at the Old Richmond Theatre on December 26. The Gibson house was on Leigh Street between Seventh and Eighth Streets, where there was a deep ravine. On the afternoon of the performance, Mrs. Gibson asked Nancy to go to Broad Street to run an errand. Upon her return, Nancy reported to Mrs. Gibson that on the way to the shop, she heard a ghost calling to her from the ravine. The ghost chanted, "Nancy, Nancy, Nancy Green, you'll die before you are sixteen." Nancy was upset and refused to go to the theatre. Mrs. Gibson convinced Nancy that to stay home would show a lack of respect for her father. Nancy, Mrs. Gibson and Mrs. McRae went to the theatre with some other friends that evening. When the fire broke out, Mrs. McRae was separated from Nancy and Mrs. Gibson, and found herself on the second floor of the building trying to escape the flames. Mrs. McRae heard a man outside call for her to jump from an open window in front of her. She jumped and the man caught her safely. Unfortunately, neither Nancy nor Mrs. Gibson made it out of the building alive. The prophecy of the ghost had indeed come true: Nancy did not live to see her sixteenth birthday.

Our tour group now exits the churchyard accompanied by the mournful sound of the iron gate. We go left and head down the steep hill along Broad Street toward Shockoe Bottom.

6.

THE CHURCH HILL TUNNEL TRAGEDY

At the corner of Broad and Eighteenth Streets, we turn left and make our way north on Eighteenth, crossing Marshall Street. About a hundred feet ahead there stands a large brick warehouse belonging to the Richmond Cold Storage Company. Just before we reach the building, we turn right and follow a set of embedded rail tracks running east. The tracks disappear into a squalid plot of ground covered with weeds, debris and brush. There, in front of us, obscured partially by a tangle of scrub trees, stands a walled-up tunnel entrance. This is a sad place, neglected and lonely. It is not the kind of place where you want to be alone at night. In fact, our regular evening tour does not usually venture this close. The concrete wall filling the arched tunnel mouth has been discolored to various shades of rust, ochre and green by the incessant trickle of water streaming down its length. This is the final resting place of locomotive 231 and the men who died around it.

In the 1870s, railroads were emerging technology. Although they had been around for many years, the rail gauge was inconsistent and track often stretched no more than one hundred miles. Astute businessmen recognized the opportunities presented by the fragmented market and began to buy up smaller railroad companies and link their tracks together. New line was added and America got a taste for how convenient it was to move people and goods by railcar. With the Civil War behind them and the economy recovering, Americans were excited to learn about the rest of the country and wanted to travel. The railroad industry was ready to explode. That was as true in Richmond as any city in the country. Richmond was an economically important city with canals going far to the west and the James River linking it to the ocean—railroads would only increase its commercial attractiveness.

Sealed entrance to the western end of the Sugar Bottom Express Line. *Photo by Jon Hood.*

Inside the tunnel next to the collapsed area showing work in progress. *Courtesy of Dementi Studios, Richmond, Virginia.*

The Chesapeake and Ohio Railroad brought an increasing amount of cargo through Richmond in the late nineteenth century. The company needed to connect east- and westbound traffic, but Church Hill stood right in the way. Going around such a large hill would require miles of track and would slow throughput. Instead, it was decided to dig a tunnel under Church Hill east from Nineteenth Street for more than four thousand feet to emerge in the area known as Sugar Bottom. Given that the hill is essentially a big lump of blue marl clay, engineers were concerned about the stability of the tunnel from the outset. The engineers had good reason to worry. During the twenty-two months it took to dig the tunnel, there were several collapses. At a cost of a dozen lives and over a million dollars, the Church Hill tunnel opened in 1873 and was used for the next several decades. With the dawning of a new century came a new steel viaduct closer to the James River and the opening of Main Street Station. C&O ceased using the tunnel in 1902.

The 1920s brought another burst of economic growth for the country and an increase in Richmond's population from returning World War I veterans who settled in the capital city. Increased trade led C&O to turn once again to the Church Hill Train Tunnel. In order for the tunnel to be useful, it needed concrete reinforcing rings, improved drainage and a general cleaning. The railroad would send a steam engine into the tunnel pulling flatcars loaded with equipment. Workers would unload the equipment and stand on the flatcars to accomplish the overhead repairs. On October 2, 1925, work was under way as over two hundred men went to work in the tunnel. The train crew and foremen were full-time employees of C&O, but the bulk of the workmen were hired as day laborers. The temporary workers would show up for work in the morning and be issued a pair of work boots. At the end of the day, they would turn in their boots to get paid.

At about 3:30 in the afternoon of October 2, Engineer Tom Mason drove steam engine number 231 and ten flatcars into the mouth at Sugar Bottom. Mason brought the train nearly all the way through the tunnel to the work site, which was only about fifty yards from the western entrance at Nineteenth Street. Shortly after the train stopped, bricks began to fall from the ceiling of the tunnel onto the tracks ahead of the locomotive. Fireman Ben Mosby called out a warning, but not quickly enough, as a tremendous cracking sound was heard above. Portions of the ceiling let go and crashed down on the train engine and the workmen. Panic ensued in the tunnel as men scrambled wildly to escape the collapsing roof. Tons of bricks and dirt crushed the boiler on the steam engine, squirting scalding steam all over Mason and Mosby. The work lights went out, plunging the workers into darkness. Men stumbled through the darkness, crying and praying, trying desperately to get out. Many of the men working toward the rear of the train were able to make their way out of the eastern entrance four thousand feet away. Others, including Mosby, crawled under the flatcars for protection and were able to get free from the rear of the train and exit to the east. As the railroad supervisors struggled to account for all of the workers, news of the tragedy spread quickly through the city. Thousands of citizens turned out to assist in the rescue effort and to see the aftermath of the collapse firsthand. Rumors spread that a large number of workers were still trapped alive in the tunnel. At the end of the day, Engineer Mason was still missing, and the count of work boots revealed that several of the laborers, including R. Lewis and H. Smith, were also unaccounted for. Fireman Mosby made it out of the tunnel, but after being taken to the hospital and relaying his account of the collapse, he died as a result of severe steam burns. The Lewis and Mason families arrived at the scene and began a vigil, clinging to the hope that their loved ones and the others trapped in the tunnel might still be discovered alive.

For eight days, a massive rescue operation continued around the clock. Rescuers knew that they had precious little time if they were going to find any of the trapped workers alive. After attempting to dig in to the tunnel from the side, the excavation crew discovered signs that the hill was sliding into the newly evacuated space, a condition exacerbated by a rainstorm on the third night. Residents in the area watched the operation closely, fearing for the safety of their homes on Church Hill. Entry from the eastern end of the tunnel was barred by the heavy, poisonous gasses that had accumulated in the wake of the collapse. Entry from the western end of the tunnel started early in the operation and continued, but little progress was made because the fragile state of the tunnel roof necessitated a completely manual digging and clearing effort. Use of a steam shovel to dig down from the top of Church Hill was abandoned when it was found that the weight of the equipment was causing further cave-ins. Ultimately, it was decided the safest way to enter the tunnel was to dig shafts directly over the estimated location of the locomotive.

On October 10, a rescue shaft reached the top of the locomotive. Hope of rescue evaporated as workers cleared away dirt to find the body of Tom Mason encased in earth that had poured in through the sides of the locomotive's cab. Mason was badly scalded by steam and the reverse lever of the locomotive had been jammed into his chest. Mason's body was removed in order to give him a proper burial. The body of Richard

Men working during the rescue effort at the western entrance. *Courtesy of Dementi Studios, Richmond, Virginia.*

Lewis was never found. Some of the men who were unaccounted for, supposedly including H. Smith, later turned up, having gotten out of the tunnel without being recorded. After a few more days, the search was called off. Since the recordkeeping was not very formal and most of the workers were day laborers, we may never know if and how many other men were killed in the collapse.

In 1926, C&O had the Church Hill tunnel filled in with sand and sealed on both ends with concrete walls. The rescue shafts were refilled and the area above was made into a park. The train and the men who died around it are still buried there today.

In the summer of 2006, the CEO of Gulf and Ohio Railways began efforts to retrieve locomotive 231 from the Church Hill tunnel. Two holes were drilled into Jefferson Hill Park over the tunnel to allow video cameras to be inserted. The search team began pumping water out of the tunnel into nearby sewers, but had not obtained the necessary permits from the City of Richmond before starting the operation. Out of concern for the possible destabilization of the hillside as a result of the water displacement and digging, the recovery effort has been at least temporarily derailed while hydrologists and engineers determine the feasibility of the operation. In the opinion of the authors, cleaning up the western end of the tunnel entrance and making it into a memorial plaza is a more suitable monument to the tragedy than removing the rusted hulk of the locomotive.

Residents of Church Hill visit Jefferson Hill Park frequently, as it offers a lovely view of the city. However, picnickers do not always enjoy their potato salad in tranquility. It seems that some of the men who died in the tunnel haven't yet found their peace. They are still trying to get out. Even in broad daylight, the muffled cries for help and pleas to "get me out" have been heard seeping up from under the ground below the park.

The Richmond Cold Storage warehouse was built right next to the western entrance to the tunnel. The building is vacant now, but when it was active, there were shifts around the clock. One gentleman who worked the graveyard shift, when the traffic outside dies down and it gets very quiet, reported hearing sounds coming from inside the tunnel. The sounds resembled those of pickaxes ringing on brick and rock. People working in the warehouse believed that what they heard was the sound of the ghosts of the laborers trying to dig their way back out of the brick-lined tunnel.

Several students from a local university heard the story of the Church Hill tunnel collapse and decided one night to go hunting for the tunnel entrance. Upon locating the entrance, the young men joked and laughed as they made their way through the undergrowth and mud guarding the tunnel mouth. The students dared each other to walk up and touch the tombstone-like concrete wall that seals the entrance. All of a sudden, the entire group stopped dead in their tracks about ten feet from the wall. The young men reported that they heard the distinctive sound of metal train wheels rolling on metal tracks, and they heard it coming from directly in front of them. Nobody touched the concrete wall that night.

While researching material for the Shadows of Shockoe tour, we came across the legend of the Richmond Vampire, which is associated with Richmond's Hollywood Cemetery. We were amazed that oral tradition had linked the tunnel collapse with the Richmond Vampire. It just goes to show that Richmond really is a small town! The following is the version of the story that we unearthed.

Many of those who first reached the Church Hill tunnel after the collapse on October 2, 1925, heroically rescued trapped men from the disaster. In some cases, rescuers at the western end of the tunnel could hear trapped workers calling for help under the huge mound of earth and with no tools at their disposal, were forced to dig in using only their bare hands. One such group ventured into the darkness of the western mouth only to stumble upon a man who was crouched down over one of the collapse victims. When the crouching man stood up, the rescue party realized that the victim on the ground was dead. The man turned to face the rescuers, and he didn't look like a tunnel worker. Neither his face nor his clothing was covered in dirt and grime, although there was a bit of blood running down his chin. As the suspicious-looking man wiped his mouth with the back of his hand, the men were mortified to see two bloody fangs protruding from his mouth. The fiend ran past the group out of the tunnel and the chase was on. The men chased the suspected vampire all the way to Hollywood Cemetery. Inside the cemetery, the vampire ran to the crypt of a man named William Waltham Pool, who had died in 1922. When the pursuers reached the Pool crypt, they found the door through which the vampire had entered was locked. Try as they might, the vampire hunters could not open the door. An appeal to the cemetery management to open the crypt was predictably declined. The story was told so widely that others went to the cemetery and attempted to gain access to the W.W. Pool crypt to see the Richmond Vampire. So many people attempted to break in to the crypt over the years that the managers of Hollywood Cemetery eventually relocated the bodies of

Mr. and Mrs. Pool to an anonymous location. Even today, the door to the crypt is chained and padlocked to prevent further vandalism.

An interesting anecdote related to the Richmond Vampire story was published in an online interview with one of Hollywood Cemetery's groundskeepers in 2005. Mr. Donald Toney, longtime grounds foreman at the cemetery, told Richmond.com that the most unusual thing he had ever witnessed in the cemetery was the discovery of a broken glass inside the locked and sealed mausoleum of W.W. Pool. Apparently, even vampires have a taste for wine every now and again.

From the Church Hill tunnel we go south on Eighteenth Street, crossing Broad Street on the way to the next stop on our tour.

7.

VIRTUOUS DANIEL IS, ALAS, NO MORE

From Broad and Eighteenth Streets, our tour group moves south down Eighteenth until we reach East Franklin Street. Facing us on the southwest corner is a restaurant called Julep's. We are looking at the oldest commercial building in Richmond—and it's haunted.

Staircases seem to feature prominently in many ghost stories. Unfortunately for us, not many good things happen on the stairs. The danger of traversing stairs is implanted in our minds at an early age as our elders stress caution while attempting to teach us to safely negotiate our way down the staircase. Who hasn't experienced the panic, pain and fear of falling down stairs with no way to regain control? In addition to our association of danger with the use of the staircase, the stairs work against our sense of security in two other ways. The image of an apparition descending a staircase to the observer's level triggers a strong predator/prey reaction. We feel vulnerable as the predator swoops down upon us. On the other hand, the sound of footsteps coming up the stairs acts as an early warning mechanism and fills us with dread at the prospect of being trapped on the upper level, unable to flee the impending danger. Whether we are above it, below it or on it, the staircase can be a scary place. For young Daniel Denoon, his final trip up the staircase of the gun shop at the corner of Eighteenth and East Franklin Streets would result in horror beyond his comprehension.

Our story begins in 1803 with the birth of Daniel Denoon. Daniel grew up in a Richmond that was experiencing a surge of tremendous growth. The population increased from less than six thousand in 1800 to over sixteen thousand by the end of the 1820s. Shockoe Bottom was the heart of the city, and new buildings and businesses were sprouting up everywhere. Tobacco and flour dominated the trade in and around the port town, but other industries such as ironworking were emerging and people were flooding in to be a part of the growth.

Julep's New Southern Cuisine restaurant in Shockoe Bottom. *Photo by Jon Hood.*

Among the many craftsmen and artisans settling in the city was a talented English gunsmith by the name of James McNaught. While Daniel Denoon grew up nearby, James McNaught opened a shop on Main Street and his skill soon caused his reputation and business to grow. The *Richmond Enquirer* described McNaught as "an admirable workman; superior to any whom we had ever had among us." In addition to the products he manufactured, McNaught also maintained his contacts back in England and imported the highest quality of firearms.

Daniel Denoon's father was a bookbinder by trade, but joined an artillery company during the War of 1812 and became a sergeant. Sergeant Denoon was killed in Canada during the Niagara campaign of 1814. Daniel's mother, distressed by the loss of her husband, looked for craftsmen who would take in her sons as apprentices. Daniel's brother became an apprentice at a brass foundry, and in 1817, the fourteen-year-old Daniel was placed in the indenture of the gunsmith James McNaught.

Daniel Denoon learned his craft well and within a few years his skills had surpassed those of his master, such that he was now considered the very best gunsmith in Virginia. James McNaught was proud of Daniel's skill and would often show off examples of his apprentice's work. McNaught sent one of Denoon's guns back to his trading partners in England, where it was pronounced to be a "master piece of its kind," according to the *Richmond Enquirer*. People liked Denoon and appreciated his skill. More and more often, customers requested his work.

By 1826, McNaught had a shop at the corner of Eighteenth and Franklin Streets in the heart of Shockoe Bottom. As was typical, he lived with his family in apartments above the shop.

Daniel stayed with McNaught for eight years, first as an apprentice and then as a foreman. As far as anyone knew, the two got along famously. They were never heard to disagree or argue. McNaught thought so highly of Denoon that he left Daniel in charge of the shop for nine months while he traveled back to England. The shop continued to prosper during this time, and McNaught promised Denoon a great reward for the job well done. That reward was never given.

At length, Daniel got an opportunity to go into business for himself. The brass founder that his brother had been apprenticed to had recently died. Daniel was considering the possibility of setting up shop in a joint venture with his brother. McNaught fought the idea, offering to take Denoon on as a partner, not just a foreman. However, as Denoon took on more responsibility for the business, McNaught's own work habits had deteriorated. The *Richmond Enquirer* reported that McNaught was "too idle, too fond of company, and it is believed, too much addicted to the bottle." McNaught thought that his partnership offer to Denoon would make up for the years of under-compensation, and that he could continue his lifestyle as he had come to enjoy it. Denoon did not openly refuse McNaught's offer, but preferred the idea of working with his brother and discouraged his master's proposition.

Late in February of 1826, a suspicious fire broke out in the gun shop. Neighbors saw the flames and were able to extinguish them before any real damage could be done. McNaught blamed the fire on the carelessness of one of the apprentices. Most people took McNaught's explanation for the fire at face value, but others knew that McNaught was heavily insured and would have received a large settlement had the building burned to the ground. Those who promulgated the rumors that McNaught set the blaze himself also insinuated that McNaught had gotten the idea that Denoon suspected him of arson.

Just three nights later, on February 27, the situation came to a head. McNaught was seen trying out various pistols throughout the day. Given his occupation, this did not seem out of the ordinary and only seemed telling after the evening's events. The McNaught family enjoyed dinner together and Denoon joined in, all seeming to have an enjoyable time. After dinner, when the family had dispersed and Denoon had gone back down to the shop, McNaught sent one of the apprentices downstairs to request that Daniel come back up for a chat. As Denoon reached the top of the stairs, McNaught approached him holding two pistols loaded with buckshot. McNaught fired the first pistol into Denoon's abdomen, causing him to stumble back down the stairs. Daniel came to rest at the foot of the staircase, mortally wounded, shocked and confused that his friend could have committed such a heinous act against him. Seconds later, the sound of the second pistol being discharged reverberated throughout the shop. McNaught had fired the pistol at his own head, but the shot only grazed his cheek, knocking him to the floor. As his blood pooled on the floor, Denoon gave a description of the event and insisted that he had no previous argument with McNaught. After a few hours, the frightened and confused Daniel Denoon passed away.

A doctor examined James McNaught. His wound was not considered critical, but in the practice of the day, he was bled from the arm. Afterward, he was conducted to the city jail and placed into a cell with some other prisoners. After the lights were put out, the guards heard a struggle coming from McNaught's bed. They entered the cell and

Daniel Denoon's tombstone in the cemetery at St. John's Episcopal Church. *Photo by Scott Bergman.*

found McNaught dead, his mattress drenched in blood and a silk scarf tied tightly around his neck. The incision in his arm where he had been bled had been torn open with a gun screw, which was found just next to his other hand. A postmortem examination was conducted, and the conclusion was reached that both the neck and arm injuries were self-inflicted, and that McNaught had bled to death. The possibility that McNaught was killed by one of the other prisoners was never seriously considered, despite the ligature marks on McNaught's neck.

Daniel Denoon's casket was given a military escort to St. John's Episcopal Church, where a multitude of friends and sympathizers attended his burial in the church cemetery. Daniel's tombstone can still be seen today with its heartfelt inscription:

> *Here lies the body of*
> *Mr. Daniel Denoon*
> *worker of this city, who was*
> *shot by James McNaught 27th Feb. 1826*
> *after being in his employ*
> *8 years, 3 months and 15 days*
> *Aged 22 years, 2 months and 15 days*
> *Lament, O ye his friends, your loss deplore*
> *For virtuous Daniel is, alas, no more*
> *And you to whom each social merit's dear,*
> *Drop o'er his grave a tributary tear*
> *For each loved attribute his soul possessed*
> *And now in Heaven enjoys eternal rest*

The building where the gun shop was located has survived to the present day and is, in fact, the oldest commercial building still standing in Richmond. The building has had many uses over the years—lumber house, soap and candle factory and various retail businesses. For a time it stood vacant. In 1995, *Style Weekly* magazine ran an article about some strange occurrences at the building. According to *Style*, two gentlemen bought the building in 1992 and began renovations to turn it into a restaurant. As a historic property, regulations required that the renovations be historically accurate. The wooden staircase where Daniel Denoon was murdered was still in place, but was so fragile as to be unsafe. The renovation plans called for replacing the staircase, but all attempts failed. With each new try, the carpenters thought they had a design that worked, but as they built it, the stairs would again be too unstable to use. During the construction, the crew returned after a weekend to find that a four-foot-tall iron safe that had been sitting in the corner near the foot of the old staircase had fallen through the floor to the basement below. The construction crew could find no obvious reason for the collapse. In addition, bricks would regularly fall from the wall at the foot of the staircase. In the *Style* article, one of the owners was quoted as saying, "It was like [the staircase] wasn't meant to be there." Eventually, a variance was granted allowing the staircase to be moved to another corner of the restaurant.

In another creepy incident, the two owners of the building stopped by one night after the crew had left just to check on things. Both owners heard what sounded like a heated exchange between two men. The sound was coming from the corner where the staircase stood. When the owners made their way to the staircase, there was no one there.

People have often reported hearing the sound of something falling or staggering downstairs when they are in the portion of the building where the old staircase once stood. Some have even reported feeling a cold spot when standing in the area where poor Daniel Denoon was murdered in cold blood over 180 years ago.

We now make our way up East Franklin to Nineteenth Street, where we will visit the first of two haunted Civil War hospitals on our tour.

8.

LASERS AND BLOOD SPOTS

Spend enough time in Virginia, and you will hear stories that nearly every old structure was once used as a hospital during the Civil War. The haunted Civil War hospital seems a cliché, and it is easy to doubt that so many commercial buildings and homes could have been used to treat casualties during the course of the war. With a little bit of research, however, it becomes painfully clear that the facts bear out the cliché: Standing at the corner of Nineteenth and East Franklin Streets, it would be difficult to throw a rock without hitting the site of a former Civil War hospital. Richmond was the destination for Confederate casualties evacuated from battlefields all throughout Virginia and points north during the war. Wounded Confederate soldiers from Manassas, the Seven Days Battles, Sharpsburg, Fredericksburg, Chancellorsville and Gettysburg, to name a few, streamed into and frequently overwhelmed the hospital system in the capital city. As the war raged on, injured Union soldiers were also brought to Richmond for treatment and incarceration.

The waves of soldiers transformed the city. To treat such vast numbers of casualties, the Confederate government leased large commercial buildings such as warehouses, factories and hotels, and converted them to hospitals. When the larger hospitals were full, churches and even private homes were put into service to accommodate the influx of those needing attention. Hundreds of thousands of soldiers moved through Richmond hospitals over the course of the war, and it was not uncommon in the aftermath of a large battle for over twenty thousand patients to be housed in the wards at one time. At the height of the war there were over one hundred hospitals operating within the city's boundaries.

During the Civil War years, the practice of medicine was still in a fairly primitive state. Fortunately for the Civil War soldier, anesthesia

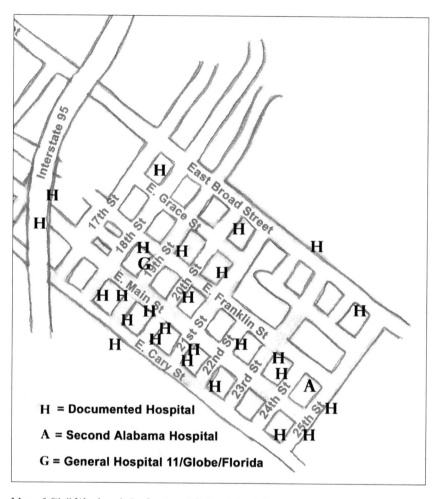

Map of Civil War hospitals. *Courtesy of Scott and Sandi Bergman.*

was generally available, making surgery tolerable. Unfortunately for the Civil War soldier, germ theory was not fully understood or accepted, and this often resulted in a lack of emphasis on sanitation and the use of antiseptics in the hospital. Wounded and diseased soldiers were kept in close quarters. Surgical instruments and bandages were reused patient after patient without sterilization. Consequently, disease and infection killed many more men than shot and shell. Given the impending onset of infection or gangrene in a wounded limb, the only choice was amputation. Often, postsurgical infections would develop and the amputee would still die a painful death. The mortality rate fluctuated greatly from hospital to hospital depending on who was in charge of the facility and how well it was staffed and supplied. The lack of available doctors, nurses and supplies put a huge strain on the hospital system and resulted in severe degradation of patient care in many hospitals. At the outset of the war, women were not allowed to serve as nurses in the wards, as they were considered too delicate for the task, not to mention the scandal of exposing their arms and necks in front of soldiers. It was not until acute manpower shortages occurred that the Confederate government was forced to accept females first as matrons, and finally as nurses.

Early in the war, the Confederate Congress passed an act that provided for the segregation of hospitals by the state from which the majority of the patients hailed. The Confederate states were each expected to supply and support the hospitals housing their native sons. The next two stops on our virtual tour bring us to the doors of the Florida hospital and one of the Alabama hospitals, where it seems that some of the patients expired but never received their furlough to the great beyond.

On Nineteenth Street, between Franklin and Main Streets, sits a three-story brick building nestled in the center of the block. This building was built in 1853 for James H. Grant to house his tobacco processing facility. In the last two decades of the nineteenth century, the building caught fire at least twice. Neither of the fires brought the whole building down—the shell survived. After each disaster, the building was rebuilt and still stands today with two original walls intact. Until 2010, 12 North Nineteenth Street was home to a laser tag company, and the upper floors were residential units.

Like many of the larger buildings in the area, 12 Nineteenth Street was pressed into service as a hospital during the Civil War. Mr. Grant's warehouse was designated General Hospital #11—sometimes called the Globe or the Florida Hospital. The Globe had a capacity of 150 patients and was in operation for more than half of the war.

In 1863, Dr. Thomas Palmer, the surgeon in charge of the Florida hospital, was so fed up with the inability to get food and supplies that he participated in the infamous bread riot on Main Street. When the mayor and governor ordered the crowd to disperse, Palmer refused to leave the scene. Palmer was charged with "unlawfully engaging in an unlawful and riotous assembly," but the charges were later dropped.

Unfortunately for the Civil War soldier, a hospital stay was often considered tantamount to a death sentence. Death in the hospitals could come suddenly and unexpectedly. The case of one Florida soldier illustrates how unpredictable the recovery process could be. Thanks to Mr. Mark Gaby for posting this information about his relative on Florida's Civil War Soldier website. Private James Jackson Nixon of Company B, Eighth Florida Regiment CSA was wounded in the hip at Culpepper, Virginia, on August 2, 1863. Private Nixon was brought to the Florida hospital in Richmond the next day, where on August 8 he dictated a letter to his wife. The letter includes the passage, "This is to inform you that my wound is still improving slowly. I am now in the Florida hospital under the best medical and surgical treatment, and hope to be able to start home in a few days. The Dr. thinks about next Wednesday or Thursday." One day later, on August 9, James Nixon died. Private Nixon was one of over a hundred men to die in the Florida hospital, despite its reputation as a clean and efficient facility.

After the war, Mr. Grant reclaimed the warehouse for his tobacco business until late in the century. Throughout the twentieth century the building was used for various retail operations, with the upper floors being various apartments, storage and office space. The configuration of the building has changed some over the years—walls added or removed, upgrades to utilities and the like, but most of the outer structure is the same as it was in the original building and is still in great shape. Over the years, people working in the building have witnessed events that may indicate some of the soldiers who died in the Florida hospital did not accompany their bodies to the grave. The sound of footsteps emanating from the upper floors and lights turned off in the evening but found on in the morning are just the beginning.

In the late 1980s, a small software firm leased space on the second floor of 12 Nineteenth Street. A programmer who worked for the company told us his firsthand encounter with the men of the Globe hospital. The programmer was working late one night and heard someone walking down the hall. Wondering which of his coworkers was also working late, the programmer got up out of his chair and walked to the door leading into the hallway. There he saw three men walking down the hall, each dressed in Confederate uniform. The trio passed by the bewildered code jockey without acknowledging his presence at all. When the three uniformed men reached the end of the hallway, they simply vanished right into the wall. The programmer decided he had worked enough for the night and beat a hasty retreat from the Globe. As it turns out, the interior wall the Confederates disappeared into was a recent addition across the original hallway. In subsequent conversations at the office, the baffled techie learned that his coworkers had frequently seen the "soldiers," especially when working in the building after nightfall. The spirits never really bothered anyone, not even seeming to be aware of the living people around them. The trio would just walk around the building as if visiting their fallen comrades.

Another company had an office upstairs. In the reception area was a spot that office workers described as the "chill spot." A small column of space, about a foot in diameter, extending from the floor to overhead, would suddenly go cold for no apparent reason. When someone walked or reached into the spot, they felt a tremendous chill. The sensation of the cold spot would only last for a few minutes before the temperature would return to normal. Some folks who experienced the chill spot also noted a feeling of melancholy that would envelope them until they moved out of the perimeter of the spot. In addition to the chill spot in the reception area, workers sometimes felt other cold spots in various places throughout the office, but the most consistent one was in the reception area. The person who relayed the phenomenon to us indicated that office workers would notice the spot in the reception area four or five times a year.

A laser tag company occupied the first floor of 12 Nineteenth Street for several years. Off the game space in the building, there is an equipment room. During game play, the door is kept locked so that guests don't find their way into the room. The game marshal—whose job it is to keep an eye on the players, assist with faulty equipment and enforce rules of play—spends a good deal of time walking around the game space. Multiple employees acting as game marshal have reported seeing the equipment door slowly slide open by itself from time to time. Inspection of the door shows that the handle is still locked, and the door just opened on its own as if pulled by an invisible hand from the inside.

The rooms in the laser tag facility that are closest to the street on the first floor are reserved for private parties. Guests can eat cake and watch the birthday boy or girl open presents in between playing laser tag games. During one party, the kids had vacated the party room to play laser tag in the arena at the rear of the building. One of the employees

General Hospital #11, as apartment building and laser tag arena. *Photo by Jon Hood.*

Sliding door that seems to open with an unseen hand. *Photo by Sandi Bergman.*

took the opportunity to do some interim cleaning in the party room. While sweeping, the young man felt someone touch him on the back. The sensation was that of being touched simultaneously by all five fingers of a hand. The employee thought that someone from the party wanted his attention, but when he turned around, there was no one in the room with him. The dutiful young man continued sweeping, and before long the hair on the back of his neck rose, as he felt the touch again. This time when he found himself alone in the room, he quickly headed back to the lobby. As the frightened young man turned a corner headed toward the lobby, he caught sight of a man standing in a back corner near one of the doors to the arena. Thinking this was one of the parents from the party waiting for the kids to come out, the young man reversed his course to tell the parent that the kids would exit the arena from a different door. The young man's already rattled constitution took another blow as the man in the corner faded from sight.

The front party room, like the others, has cinder block walls and cement floors. The floors currently in place are old, but not as old as other parts of the building. When the laser tag company moved in, the floors were quite dirty with grime and tar from years of wear and tear. As part of the cleanup and decorating effort, the floors were cleaned and painted. The floor in the party room cleaned up nicely and started off with a light, uniform color across the entire surface. However, after a few days the workers noticed a discolored spot on the floor near the front window. Each day the spot grew larger and more distinct until it clearly showed reddish brown over the paint. The maintenance staff painted over the spot, and the floor was once again a uniform color. A few days later, the reddish brown spot returned, causing people to start referring to the discoloration as a "blood spot." The frustrated maintenance staff cleaned the spot with a floor cleanser and then went back through the paint-clear, spot-returns cycle. The cycle was repeated for several iterations, using many different cleansers, including bleach. Every time, the spot returned. Finally, the laser tag company took drastic measures by sanding down about a quarter inch of the cement from the floor, covering it with concrete patch, sealing and painting it. You can guess what happened. It may have played out like a comedy of errors, but the management of the laser tag company finally accepted its role as Lady Macbeth in the tragedy being presented in the Globe as an open-ended run for all eternity.

From the Florida hospital, our tour resumes the trek east down Franklin Street toward the site of another former Civil War hospital.

9.

GHOSTS OF THE
SECOND ALABAMA HOSPITAL

We first met Peter at a neighborhood association meeting. We had heard some stories and read the article in *Style Weekly* magazine about the reports of paranormal activity in the Pohlig Box Factory apartment building, but going into the meeting we had no idea that we would get a firsthand account from the guy featured in the article. After hearing us announce the Shadows of Shockoe Ghost Tour, Peter approached us after the meeting and told us he had some inside information on the Pohlig building. We were all ears, and with Peter, we headed off to one of the fine establishments in Shockoe Bottom to take in his story over a pint of ale. We were excited, because we knew that the building known as the Pohlig Box Factory was once the home of a Civil War hospital.

In Richmond during the Civil War, the state of Alabama opened four hospitals for the care of its soldiers. Financed by the state treasury and private donations, the Alabama hospitals were made possible in large part due to the tremendous effort of Juliet O. Hopkins, who served as administrator, matron, fundraiser and donor.

It is to the site of the Second Alabama Hospital located at Twenty-fifth and Franklin Streets that our tour now proceeds. At the intersection we see a large industrial-looking red brick building with two black-and-white signs painted directly on the wall between rows of whitewashed window frames. The upper sign reads "POHLIG BROS.," and the lower sign reads "MANUFACTURERS OF PAPER BOXES." This is the building that housed the Second Alabama Hospital from 1861 to 1863.

The building dates back to 1853 and was originally a tobacco factory known as the Yarborough Turpin Factory. In 1861, the factory made room for the Alabama hospital, yielding space on the main floor for surgeons and administrators and space on the upper floors to house approximately two hundred men.

Mrs. Hopkins's accounting indicated that about 3,700 patients came through the Second Alabama Hospital, with 300 soldiers dying there. The Second Alabama Hospital was closed as part of an overall reorganization in 1863, but was again used to treat casualties in some of the later battles of the war, including Union casualties.

After the war, Yarborough and Turpin reclaimed the factory and resumed their tobacco business. In 1909, Pohlig Bros., Inc. purchased the Yarborough Turpin Tobacco Factory building and converted it into a paper box factory. The box factory operated there until 1992, when it relocated, leaving the building vacant. The building has since been renovated to house luxury apartments. The Pohlig Box Factory is a popular address in the Tobacco Row area and many of the apartments come with amenities that aren't listed in the brochure, as we learned from our conversation with Peter from the neighborhood association.

As we sipped our beer, Peter told us the story of a night, or a portion of a night, he spent in the Pohlig Box Factory Building. Peter was dating a young lady who rented one of the apartments at Pohlig, and he was staying over for the night. His side of the bed was several feet from the bedroom wall. A bicycle leaned against the wall on Peter's side of the bed. The kickstand on the bike was down, facing the bed. According to Peter, the bicycle was arranged such that if it fell it would either be caught by the kickstand or would hit the ground without making contact with the bed. Peter told us he was lying on his side with his back to the wall about to fall asleep when he felt the bicycle fall against him. It seemed odd to him that the bike hit the bed, but he simply pushed the bike away and tried once again to go to sleep. Just a few minutes later, he had the sensation of fingernails scratching down his back. The sensation started at the base of his neck and continued all the way down the spine to his lower back, taking what seemed to Peter like an entire minute. Peter said he was paralyzed with fear and did not move for almost an hour. His girlfriend slept through the entire event. Eventually, Peter got up, got dressed and made up an excuse about an early meeting, leaving the apartment. He said he never stayed over again in the apartment. Not wanting to upset his girlfriend, Peter didn't tell her the story until after she had moved out. Peter's girlfriend told him that she never experienced anything abnormal while she was living in the Pohlig Box Factory Building.

A tenant in the Pohlig Box Factory apartments went on the Shadows of Shockoe Ghost Tour one night and told this story: He was in his bedroom sleeping one night when he suddenly awoke. He couldn't remember later if he had heard a sound or felt some sort of change in the room that roused him. The man told us he wasn't even sure if he was fully awake, but when he opened his eyes he saw a room full of people. He said it was almost like a waiting room—people standing, sitting, walking around. Some talked to each other, and some sat by themselves. The people didn't seem threatening to the man and apparently didn't notice his presence. The sight of people all around his room upset the man quite a bit, but at first he was still too groggy to move and just watched them. As he began to realize his own fear and awoke fully, all of the people he had seen in the room vanished.

The following secondhand stories about the Pohlig Box Factory were collected from guests on the Shadows of Shockoe Ghost Tour. It is worth mentioning that the Pohlig Box Factory remains a very popular place to live, and most residents have not experienced any paranormal activity while living there.

A woman lived in an apartment by herself and had never experienced anything unusual. One night, her boyfriend stayed over, and sometime after they went to sleep a thunderstorm moved into the area. In the middle of the night the woman was awakened by a loud thunderclap. The woman groggily glanced toward a window just as lightning flashed outside. She saw the figure of a man standing in front of the window. Assuming it was her boyfriend standing at the window, she tried to go back to sleep. A moment later, another bolt of lightning illuminated the window and the figure was still there. By this time, the woman was fully awake and so she called to her boyfriend to find out why he was standing at the window. The woman was startled when her boyfriend responded from beside her in the bed! Now terrified, the woman quickly turned on the light to see who was standing in front of the window, and there was no one there, or anywhere else in the apartment. Was it a shadow, or was it a Confederate soldier from Alabama?

A resident who lived in the Pohlig Box Factory Building with her young daughter was interested in the spirits who have been said to walk the halls. One night the mother had some friends over after putting her daughter to bed. The friends had set up for a séance and were getting under way when the little girl came down the hallway in her pajamas and politely asked her mother where the man in her bedroom had gone. No guests had left the living room, and none of the guests were men. The little girl was not frightened, but curious about her visitor. He hadn't said anything, but had smiled at her and then walked away.

An executive who lived alone was in her apartment at Pohlig Box Factory one night catching up on some paperwork for her job. She was stretched out on her bed leaning against the headboard. The woman was

Pohlig Box Factory apartment building, where the unfortunate patients of the Second Alabama Hospital wander still. *Photo by Jon Hood.*

facing a dresser that stood against the opposite wall. On the dresser was a small dish for spare change. The woman was engrossed in what she was reading when she heard a strange sound. Looking around the room she didn't see anything at first, but heard the sound again. Zeroing in on the location of the noise, she sat up and looked at the dresser. There she saw the change moving, one coin at a time, sliding out of the dish, onto the dresser, then over to the edge and dropping to the floor. Once on the floor, the coins would stop moving. Coin after coin slid to the edge and dropped until the dish was empty. The woman was paralyzed with fear. She could see nothing in the vicinity of the dresser that could explain the movement of the coins. The frightened woman found another place to stay the night, and soon afterward, she moved out of the building.

An employee of the Pohlig Box Factory apartments reported that there was one particular apartment that just would not rent. The apartment looked similar to others in the building and didn't have a particularly poor view or location in relation to its neighbors. But whenever this apartment was shown, prospective tenants didn't seem interested, some even reporting a "bad feeling" while they were inside. The apartment had other peculiarities, such as an exterior hallway light that would turn on unexpectedly and cabinet doors that wouldn't stay closed. Whenever the apartment was shown, the cabinet doors in the kitchen would be open. Even when an agent planned to show the apartment and made sure the doors were closed ahead of the appointment, when that agent returned for the showing, the doors would be open again.

While none of the Pohlig Box Factory stories specifically identify Civil War soldiers as the ghosts that haunt the building, the backstory of the Second Alabama Hospital and the hundreds of Confederate soldiers who died on the site certainly provides a compelling reason for paranormal activity on the premises.

Perhaps it is not the trauma of the Alabama soldiers' deaths that makes them restless after all. Instead, it could be the proximity of the Second Alabama Hospital to the site of the abode of an infamous Union spy. From the Pohlig Box Factory, we backtrack down Franklin to North Twenty-third Street and turn right to climb the hill on the way to "Crazy Bet's" stomping grounds.

10.

CRAZY BET'S STOMPING GROUNDS

Our next stop is an elementary school located on the site where a lovely old mansion once stood. Admittedly, this site has the sketchiest ghost stories associated with it, but the story of the colorful and controversial character who inhabited the mansion during the latter half of the nineteenth century makes it worth a stop on our tour. We head up Church Hill on North Twenty-third Street. We stop at the intersection of North Twenty-third and East Grace Streets. Bellevue Elementary School is on our right facing Grace Street.

One day, a group of girls gathered inside the school, preparing for an after-school activity. When the group walked passed the school theatre, they noticed it was dark. A mischievous girl in the group dared another girl to go from the door at the entrance of the theatre all the way down to the stage and touch it before coming back out. The little girl who had been challenged thought about it a moment, and then accepted the dare. The brave little girl made her way into the pitch black theatre and began the long journey to the stage. She was about halfway to her destination when some movement on the stage caught her attention and arrested her progress. The little girl could make out the shadowy figure of a woman walking slowly but purposefully across the stage from one side toward the other. The little girl said that she could clearly see the woman, even though it was dark in the theatre. Before the female form reached the far side of the stage, it vanished.

In the greenroom, where performers wait while they are not onstage, a peculiar noise is sometimes heard. The sound is a rhythmic creaking of wood. People have gone to great lengths to search out the source of this noise. The sound has been heard when the room is full of people and when only one person is there. Faculty members have searched in the

Bellevue Elementary School, which is on the site of the former Adams-Van Lew Mansion. *Photo by Jon Hood.*

crawl spaces, in cabinets and closets, but cannot find anything that might account for the sound. When asked to describe what they heard, most people describe it as the sound of a chair rocking on a hardwood floor.

Are these incidents actually encounters with the ghost of Elizabeth Van Lew, also known as "Crazy Bet"?

Elizabeth Van Lew was born in Richmond in 1818 to John and Eliza Van Lew. John was a wealthy man, having made his fortune as a hardware merchant. In 1829, Mr. Van Lew purchased a Greek Revival mansion on Church Hill that had been built in 1801. The family moved in and Elizabeth lived there until her death in 1900. The family was popular in the city and entertained Richmond's society in their beautiful mansion. Such prominent citizens as John Marshall were known to have visited for dinner. Edgar Allan Poe once gave a reading of his poem "The Raven" in the parlor of the Van Lew mansion.

Elizabeth was considered intelligent and attractive and was well known and well liked as a young girl. She was part of Richmond society and made friends with young ladies in other families of equivalent social stature. Once she reached young adulthood, Elizabeth was sent to Philadelphia to attend finishing school. It was in Philadelphia that she met a young teacher who was an ardent abolitionist. Elizabeth was greatly influenced by the teacher and took on the cause as her own. Not long after she returned to Richmond, Elizabeth's father died after being in ill health for several years. Upon his death, John Van Lew left the house and most of his fortune to his wife, but also left a substantial inheritance to each of his three children. Elizabeth's younger brother and sister eventually moved out of the house, but Elizabeth and her mother continued to live there.

Elizabeth was a bold woman and strong in her convictions. She was intelligent and able to argue convincingly. Prior to the outbreak of the Civil War, the slavery issue was hotly debated, even in the city of Richmond—as was the issue of secession. Elizabeth was outspoken in her positions against both slavery and secession.

Elizabeth convinced her mother to free the family's remaining slaves and began using her inheritance to buy slaves, set them free and send them north. These actions made her increasingly unpopular in Richmond, but it was her behavior during the war that finally made her a social outcast in the capital of the Confederacy. It is interesting to note the extent to which Elizabeth's subversive activity went unnoticed. Richmond was such a tight-knit community that it must have been unthinkable that one of the daughters in such an upstanding Southern family could side with the despised Yankees.

Elizabeth Van Lew. *Courtesy of Virginia State Library.*

As soon as Union prisoners of war started arriving in Richmond, Elizabeth and her mother began to visit them. While most "good Richmonders" were visiting the wounded Confederates, Elizabeth was visiting Union soldiers in the newly opened Libby Prison on Cary Street. Elizabeth quickly recognized that she needed to appear harmless to the Confederate guards, or she might be denied access to the prisoners. That's when Elizabeth took on the persona of "Crazy Bet." She began to dress as a commoner (something ladies in her social circle did not do), wearing buckskin trousers and calico bonnets. She would walk down the street singing silly songs out loud to herself. Elizabeth's status as an unmarried woman in her forties only served to reinforce the idea that she was mentally unbalanced. Initially, the Libby Prison guards were suspicious of Elizabeth's frequent visits to the Yankee prison, and even turned her away on one occasion. Elizabeth rectified the situation by bringing a home-cooked dessert, ostensibly for the prisoners, and leaving the platter with the Confederate officer in charge. Well-timed generosity and the affected "Crazy Bet" personality did the trick, and she rarely had trouble getting access to Union prisoners of any rank held in the Richmond prisons.

Elizabeth's compassion for the Union soldiers made her one of the most despised women in the city. But along with food and sympathy, Elizabeth also brought information to the Union prisoners. She exchanged sensitive information by passing encrypted notes back and forth in the spines of books that she brought into the prisons. In this way she was able to maintain a steady stream of current information between Union prisoners and the United States military command.

Over the course of the war, Elizabeth Van Lew developed an elaborate network of spies and was able to communicate valuable information quickly. The messages she sent went all the way to General Ulysses S. Grant. After the war, the general praised Elizabeth for the timeliness and value of the information she provided. Van Lew's covert communication methods were often crafty. For example, she would use hollowed out eggshells or slits in the soles of shoes to conceal notes. Remarkably, she was never caught in the act of passing these messages.

Elizabeth corresponded with the families of prisoners, informing them of the condition of their loved ones. She also kept up a written correspondence with her dear "uncle," Mr. James Jones. As it turned out, Uncle James was actually a ruse for messages sent to Federal officers outside of Confederate lines. When the seemingly innocuous letters were subjected to heat, invisible ink showed the true messages written between the lines of the faux letter.

Libby Prison, where Van Lew visited and shared information with the Union soldiers.
Courtesy of Virginia State Library.

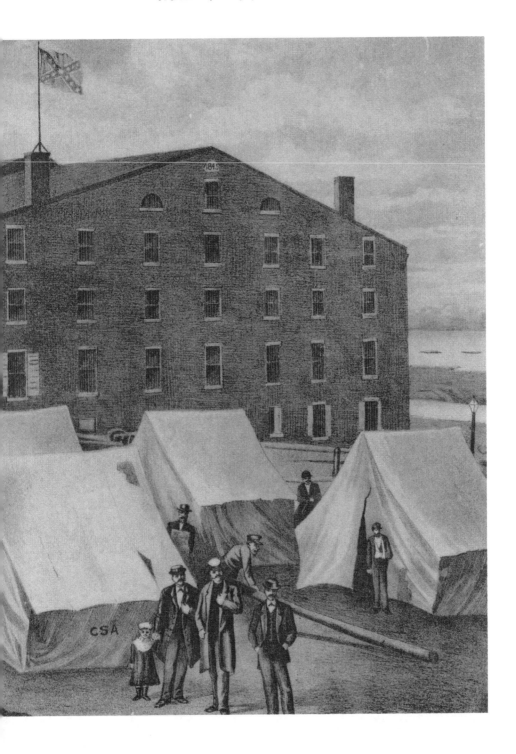

Ulrich Dahlgren led an ill-fated attempt to release the prisoners at Libby and attack the city. The idea for the attempt was said to have originated with Elizabeth Van Lew. *Courtesy of Virginia State Library.*

Van Lew's spy network included one of the young, free black women whom Elizabeth had arranged to send north to get an education. Van Lew convinced the young woman to play the role of an uneducated servant and arranged for her spy to work in the home of Confederate President Jefferson Davis. Elizabeth's spy was able to gather critical information from meetings that were held in the White House of the Confederacy.

One of Elizabeth's most impressive feats was arranging the secret relocation of the body of Union Colonel Ulrich Dahlgren, the leader of a failed Federal raid on Richmond late in the war. Some say that Elizabeth Van Lew originated the plan. Dahlgren was to lead a contingent of Federal troops south across the James River west of the city and then descend upon the prisoner of war camp at Belle Isle, releasing the prisoners and then attacking the city if possible. The plan went awry when the Union forces discovered that the targeted crossing point in the river was too swollen from floodwaters to be forded. The raiding party of about five hundred men was forced to backtrack and was engaged by Confederate forces and the Richmond Home Guard. The Union soldiers were trapped and almost half of them were killed, including their leader, Ulrich Dahlgren. When Confederate troops recovered Dahlgren's corpse, they found the plan for the raid and made the details public. The thought of vengeful Union prisoners terrorizing the capital enraged the citizens of Richmond. In a show of disrespect, one of Dahlgren's fingers was cut off and his wooden leg was taken off his corpse. Dahlgren's body was buried in an unmarked grave, ostensibly to prevent further desecration of the body. Elizabeth Van Lew was able to discover the location of Dahlgren's makeshift grave and arrange to have the body reburied on the farm of a fellow Union sympathizer. The original grave was refilled, and the theft was not discovered until weeks later when the Confederates agreed to return Dahlgren's remains to the Union army. When no coffin was found in the unmarked grave, the Confederates were stumped. It wasn't until after the war that Van Lew contacted Dahlgren's family so that they could transfer Colonel Dahlgren's remains to their final resting place in the family cemetery in Philadelphia.

Elizabeth's brother John shared her support for the Union cause. Late in the war, however, he was conscripted into the Confederate army. He only lasted a few weeks before he deserted after the Battle of Cold Harbor and holed up in one of Elizabeth's many safe houses. It has been rumored that Van Lew often used her own house as a refuge for Unionists and escaped prisoners. The discovery of secret rooms in her mansion after her death lends weight to these stories. Rumors have surfaced from time to time that the Van Lew mansion was a stop on the Underground

Adams-Van Lew Mansion. *Courtesy of Virginia State Library.*

Railroad, but these have not been confirmed. It was while she was visiting her brother one night, just after his desertion, that she received word of a massive prisoner escape from Libby Prison. Elizabeth knew that such an escape was planned and offered her network of safe houses to be used as way stations for the escapees. Elizabeth and her brother John spent a tense night expecting the Confederate soldiers to burst in at any time, but the network held and once again her involvement went undetected.

After the war, Elizabeth was highly praised by those on the side of the Union, but loathed by those on the side of the Confederacy. Her neighbors and acquaintances wanted nothing to do with her. Elizabeth had lost her fortune over the course of the war due to staggering inflation and her efforts to buy freedom for slaves. Some of the prisoners she had assisted during the war helped to support her financially when she fell on hard times. When Ulysses S. Grant became president of the United States, he appointed Elizabeth Van Lew postmistress of Richmond, a position she held for many years. Elizabeth had carried out her "Crazy Bet" charade so effectively that many people still thought of her as a crazy old woman. Despite efforts in her later years to ingratiate herself with neighbors by hosting parties and inviting folks to her house, Elizabeth was never really accepted back into Richmond society. Elizabeth died a social outcast in 1900.

Elizabeth was buried in the Van Lew family plot at Shockoe Cemetery. Her admirers in the North provided a marker for her grave. The marker is a granite boulder bearing a bronze plaque that includes the epitaph, "She risked everything that is dear to man—friends, fortune, comfort, health, life itself, all for the one absorbing desire of her heart, that slavery might be abolished and the Union preserved." Elizabeth Van Lew was a remarkable woman who demonstrated that sometimes there is a high price to pay for living true to one's convictions.

The Virginia Club purchased the Van Lew mansion, and in 1911 it was demolished to make way for the construction of Bellevue Elementary School. Perhaps the mysterious figure seen at Bellevue Elementary is that of Crazy Bet, wandering around her old stomping grounds and sitting in her rocking chair waiting for the neighbors to drop in and pay her a visit.

From the site where Edgar Allan Poe once recited his poem "The Raven," we go back down Twenty-third Street on our way to the building that now houses the Poe Museum. But before we even get there, we are obligated to point out that Poe never lived in the building we are about to visit! We head south on Twenty-third to Main Street and turn right on our way to the Old Stone House.

11

THE CHILDREN OF
THE OLD STONE HOUSE

It is a beautiful fall afternoon in the Enchanted Garden at the Edgar Allan Poe Museum located at 1914 East Main Street, just a few blocks east of the 17th Street Farmers' Market. The bride and groom beam at each other as they cut the wedding cake and share it with their jubilant guests. It is hard to imagine a more tranquil spot in the city than the courtyard located behind the oldest building still standing in the city of Richmond. Known simply as the Old Stone House, the structure serves as the centerpiece of the Poe Museum. The click of the photographer's camera and the whir of the video camera can be heard as images of the festive occasion are captured for posterity. The sounds of lively discussion, a string quartet, laughter and the gentle trickling of a fountain reverberate against the brickwork that frames the courtyard and makes up the grotto at the rear of the lot. In a corner of the yard, a young girl and boy contentedly play on the fringes of the vibrant party. The youngsters look on as the party proceeds, but they keep to themselves and do not approach any of the adults at the party. They are content in their own little world.

The scene in the Enchanted Garden of the Poe Museum sounds like a typical outdoor wedding party. It is, with one exception. None of the guests at the party have children with them. These are the children of the Old Stone House, and they are ghosts.

Although the exact date that the Old Stone House was built is unknown, City of Richmond property records list the year as 1737. The Association for the Preservation of Virginia Antiquities cites the use of dendrochronology, commonly known as tree ring dating, to date the house to around 1754.

The house itself is made of nonuniform building stones and stands one and a half stories high with a gabled, dormered roof. The original plan may be described as a hall-parlor arrangement. The house sits on the north side of Main Street, facing south. Although neighboring buildings are

The Enchanted Garden behind the Poe Museum, where you might see the children playing. *Photo by Sandi Bergman.*

still relatively small for the heart of a major city, there is no doubt that the stone house stands out as an artifact from another era. In fact, it is said to be the only colonial-era family dwelling still standing in the city of Richmond.

German silversmith Jacob Ege owned the property in 1742 when the town was incorporated as a city by William Byrd II. Jacob and his wife Maria were the progenitors of a family that would retain possession of the Old Stone House into the early part of the twentieth century.

Samuel Ege, son of Jacob and Maria, was a prominent Richmonder who lived with his family in the Old Stone House for many years in the late eighteenth century. It is Samuel's name that appears as the owner of the house on the first known document referring to the property. Not surprisingly, this was a tax document, from the year 1782. Samuel was a flour inspector, a position of great importance in a city reliant on the high quality of products leaving its ports. Flour was the second largest export from the city of Richmond, behind tobacco. By harnessing the power of the James River to build powerful mills, Richmond was on its way to becoming the largest exporter of flour in the world. With the boom in commerce, the Ege family prospered.

The Ege family would come to own a great deal of property around Richmond's riverfront area, including partial ownership of the building that would later become the infamous Libby Prison during the Civil War. The descendants of the Eges owned the Old Stone House and the lot it sits on until 1911.

Over the years the house has been the subject of many stories, some of which are verifiable and some of which are highly unlikely. Rumors of Native American graves on the property were circulated for years—most likely the earliest ghost stories associated with the house. The sheer age of the house makes it a magnet for attachment to the names of many famous visitors to Richmond who are said to have stopped at the house for one reason or another.

It is reliably reported that James Monroe boarded at the Old Stone House during the convention of 1788. One of the Ege family descendants reminisced about hearing her grandparents tell of visits by Thomas Jefferson and James Madison. For years, it was said that the Old Stone House served as headquarters for George Washington during the Revolutionary War. The house appears in postcards from the 1860s and 1870s showing a sign proclaiming that honor. While the house was certainly standing in Richmond during the Revolutionary War, General Washington was not. Little fighting took place around Richmond, although the city was burned to the ground in 1781 by a British force under the command of

Benedict Arnold. Washington spent very little if any of his time in the city of Richmond during the war. Instead, Washington dispatched the Marquis de Lafayette to Richmond to prevent a second British incursion. Lafayette took on Arnold at the Battle of Petersburg, preventing another attack on Richmond and winning the hearts of Richmonders for generations. The Marquis de Lafayette is said to have visited the residents of the stone house during his grand tour of Richmond in 1824. Evidence exists that Lafayette may have been escorted to the property by none other than a young Edgar Allan Poe. At the tender age of fifteen, Poe was a member of the Junior Morgan Rifleman Volunteers. The unit was organized as a military honor guard assigned to the Lafayette procession.

Apparently, there is no evidence that Edgar Allan Poe himself spent appreciable time in the Old Stone House. Given the proximity of the house to several sites that figured prominently in Poe's life, there is a decent chance that the famous writer may have visited the landmark on occasion.

Poe's mother, Elizabeth, was an actor. She moved to Richmond in 1810 and performed frequently at the Old Richmond Theatre, which was located on the north side of Broad Street, facing Capitol Hill. Elizabeth Poe died of tuberculosis in December of 1811, when Edgar was only two years old. The Old Richmond Theatre burned to the ground just weeks after her death, claiming seventy-two lives. Monumental Church was built on the site of the theatre, and it is believed that Edgar Allan Poe attended services at the church on occasion. Elizabeth Poe is buried in the cemetery of St. John's Episcopal Church, about a mile away from Monumental Church. St. John's is the church where Patrick Henry delivered his famous "Give me liberty, or give me death" speech.

Elizabeth Poe's death left young Edgar an orphan. At the time of Elizabeth's death, David Poe Jr., Edgar's father, had disappeared from the record, possibly dying in 1810. The prominent Allan family of Richmond took in young Edgar as a foster child. Poe's childhood homes with the Allans were located just a handful of blocks from the Old Stone House along Main Street, with the best known being Moldavia at Fifth and Main Streets.

The Craig House, located at East Grace and Nineteenth Streets, was the home of Jane Stith Craig Stanard, mother of Richard Stanard, one of Poe's schoolmates. Mrs. Stanard was the inspiration for Poe's famous poem "To Helen."

Between 1835 and 1837, Edgar Allan Poe served as writer, critic and editor at the *Southern Literary Messenger*, located at Fifteenth and Main Streets. The *Messenger* was a prominent literary magazine during the early

The Poe Museum, Richmond, Virginia. *Photo by Jon Hood.*

half of the nineteenth century, and Poe was partially responsible for the rapid increase in circulation during the years that he worked there. While working at the *Southern Literary Messenger*, Poe lived in a boardinghouse on Bank Street, opposite Capitol Square.

In 1911, the Association for the Preservation of Virginia Antiquities purchased the Old Stone House at auction. For a decade, the house was vacant or served as a small shop. In 1922, a group that would become the Poe Foundation purchased the house and property as a place to build a Poe Shrine. It has been the home of the Edgar Allan Poe Museum ever since. When the *Southern Literary Messenger* Building was demolished in 1915, materials from the building were used in the construction of the Poe Shrine and garden. Another small house was built in the front of the property right next to the Old Stone House. Bricks from the *Messenger* Building were also used in the construction of this building. The second house on the property was used to hold some of the museum's expanding collections. A small house sitting directly west of the Old Stone House obscured part of the old edifice, and so the front rooms were removed from that house in order to have a better view of the historic home from the street. Finishing out the campus is another small brick house in the back corner of the lot, which was also acquired by the Poe Museum to house collections.

The setting of the Poe Shrine and garden is lovely and is almost completely surrounded by buildings, making it a quiet venue in the heart of a bustling city. The garden is often used for special occasions such as weddings, luncheons and parties. After some of these events, odd things have been reported. Guests have called the museum to let them know that their videos, which showed no problems during the event, go black at times when the house comes into view, only to show a full picture again once the house is out of the frame. A bride once called the museum to report a problem with her wedding pictures. The wedding party was situated so that the house was in the background of the pictures. The photographer had taken several versions of each shot to be sure to get at least one good photo of all members in the party. Most of the pictures turned out beautifully, but a few of the pictures show a round, bright white spot in the middle of the group. The photographer assured the bride that it couldn't be sun glare, and that he had never had anything like that happen to his camera.

But what about the children?

From time to time, guests inquire about the children they see playing in the corner of the garden during an event. The children don't do anything to the guests or attempt to join the festivities; they just play happily off in a corner. They are noticed by someone, but when that person looks back to see where they are, the children have vanished. The two youths are described as a little boy and little girl who bear a resemblance to one another. The guests who report this insist the children are not part of their group. Museum staff monitors the entrance of the house during private events, and would certainly know if anyone uninvited entered.

It is the museum staff that most frequently sees evidence of the children. A docent was giving a tour one weekend and was wrapping it up in the downstairs entry hall of the house at the front corner of the lot. Because she is a diminutive person, she stepped up to the second stair so that her group could see her better. Just as she was finishing her speech, there was the sound of a crash from overhead. All members of the tour looked up when they heard it. The guide knew that there was no one upstairs, so she quickly finished the tour, ushered the guests out of the house, called to the other docent on duty and together they went back to see what had happened. Upstairs, a table had been overturned and its contents strewn across the floor. A brief inspection revealed that no permanent damage had been done, so the two docents set about putting the table display back in order. While the two women were working, both said that they heard the distinct sound of giggling from the corner of the room.

On one of the Shadows of Shockoe Ghost Tour routes, the small carriage house in the rear of the Poe Museum lot is the first building in the museum complex that comes into view. On one occasion, the tour group stopped behind the carriage house while the tour guide answered a question about the Poe Museum. As the guide was speaking, a member of the tour snapped a picture of one of the rear windows using a digital camera. On the image, there appeared to be something in the carriage house window. After going home and looking at a larger version of the photo on a computer monitor, the guest saw what looked like a small face looking out of the window. Several guests on subsequent tours have snapped pictures of the carriage house window showing the same odd phenomenon. Is it one of the children peeking at the members of the ghost tour?

Inside the Old Stone House, the museum gift shop and front desk occupy the largest room downstairs. The other room is display space, and the small rooms upstairs are used mostly for storage these days. People working the front desk sometimes hear footsteps overhead. Of course, the old house is not well insulated and creaks like a—well, an old house, but the workers in question say that they hear the definite sounds of footsteps. At times, museum staff members have walked

House built to display the Poe collections. Faces are seen in the second-story windows. *Photo by Sandi Bergman.*

Back bedroom where a little boy's footsteps are heard. *Photo by Sandi Bergman.*

upstairs to catch sight of a small boy in the back bedroom. The staff members report that the boy is wearing knee pants and a light-colored shirt. The little boy is a shy ghost and disappears as soon as he realizes he has been seen. Most people believe he is the one whose footsteps are occasionally heard. This coy little boy may also be responsible for moving things around in the gift shop. The staff will sometimes come in to find that items on the shelves have been moved around. It doesn't happen very often, and it is not that things go missing; they're just in a different place in the morning than they were when the doors were locked the night before.

One day, one of the docents brought his daughter to work with him. She had homework, and she had brought her clarinet and several pieces of music to practice. The docent's daughter spent several hours working upstairs in the storage room, but then grew bored and left her things to go and find her father. The girl left her clarinet standing up on a desk, sitting on top of her stacked sheet music. When the girl returned to collect her things to go home, the clarinet had been knocked over and the music sheets spread across the desk.

A supervisor of the museum, who won't say specifically whether he believes all of the stories of the children of the Old Stone House, does tell of a rather creepy experience he once had at the museum. One of the back doors to the Old Stone House hangs such that when it swings open fully, it will come in contact with an interior wall. If pushed hard, it will bang into the wall with a loud thump. The supervisor has been

A postcard of the Old Stone House. *Courtesy of Scott Bergman.*

working at the museum long enough to be used to this and is careful when he opens the door. However, one day the door got away from him as he was entering the house and slammed with a mighty knock into the wall. As the supervisor was standing there, he heard an answering knock from the other side of the wall. The spot where the second knock seemed to emanate is not accessible from inside the house—this space being a small cavity inside the wall. Curious as to what might have caused the knock, the supervisor knocked on the wall again, this time just using his hand. Again there was an answering knock. He tried again, knocking twice. There came two answering knocks. The answering knocks sounded like someone on the inside of the wall knocking with his or her bare knuckles. Perplexed, but still curious, he tried three knocks. When he got three knocks back from the other side, he decided he wasn't going to play the game anymore and whatever was knocking would just have to find another playmate. The supervisor has not heard the knocking again, and has never been able to find an explanation for the first incident.

And so we leave the Old Stone House, with the sensation of eyes peering at us from the dormer windows as we leave the children behind. Will we ever know who the children of the Old Stone House are? Or perhaps they will remain, in the words of Poe, "Nameless here for evermore." And when will someone once again hear the gentle rapping, the persistent tapping near the back door? It may also be as the Raven remarked: "Nevermore."

Our tour now makes its way west down Main Street into the hopping nightlife district between Seventeenth and Eighteenth Streets.

12.

MYSTERY ON MAIN STREET

It was late one night in February of 2006. Two painters were just finishing their work in one of the second-story rooms at 1718 East Main Street. The building, which was built in 1914, had most recently housed a series of nightclubs before standing empty for several months. It was now about to reopen as Big Daddy's Sports Club. The owner and several workers had been working over the course of the winter to refurbish the place in time for a spring opening. This put just a few people working in the building for fairly long periods of time, as was the case on that February evening. A boom box in the corner of the room played music broadcast from a local radio station. The two painters moved their paint cans, equipment and drop cloths into the next room to start painting there. The men could easily hear the music in the second room, so they left the stereo behind in the first room and began to work. After a few moments, the radio suddenly switched to another station. The change was abrupt—as though someone had pressed a preset button to switch the station. The two men were sure that they were the only ones in the building, but they called out to see if anyone had entered without them noticing. No reply—just the sound of the newly changed radio station. With a great deal of curiosity, the painters went into the room with the stereo. They checked out the radio, but it was sitting as they left it with no obvious signs of tampering. They put it back on the station they had been listening to and went back to work. Neither man thought much of the incident at the time, but it is a pretty good bet that they were listening much more closely to the radio for the rest of that evening.

This first strange occurrence did not spark thoughts of a ghost, but rather more of a gremlin. As is the case with many haunted places, it isn't until incidents start to add up that people begin to suspect the

A modern-day picture of the restaurant that currently resides in this building. *Photo by Jon Hood.*

Main Street from Twentieth Street looking west. *Courtesy of Virginia State Library.*

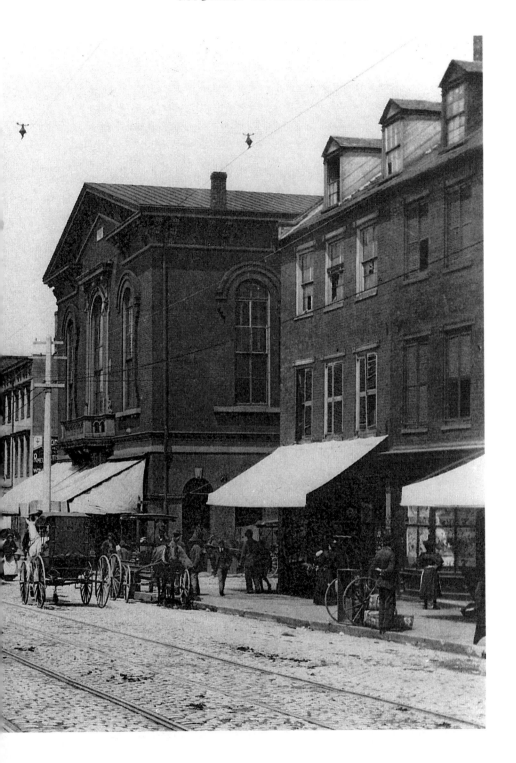

paranormal. Two days after the radio incident, something else happened that made the workers change their thinking. The three men working that day were preparing to leave and they did their routine check of all the doors to ensure they were locked. As they were walking out the front door, they heard the sound of the upstairs ladies' room door closing. That door does not swing freely, so it makes a distinctive sound when it is closed. The men weren't thinking ghosts at all this time; they thought someone had gotten into the building to spend the night. The three of them rushed upstairs to see who it was, but when they opened the door to the ladies' room and looked inside, it was empty. The workers quickly searched the rest of the building and found no other living souls inside. After their fruitless search, the men began to entertain the idea of an otherworldly presence in the building. After that night, they began to pay more attention to the noises they heard in the building as they were working. The buildings on either side were empty at the time, so when all the people in the work party were in the room together and they heard noises in another part of the building, they knew it was the ghost. Lights would turn on and off seemingly by themselves, and the workers would discover their tools moved from the places where they remembered leaving them. The club finally opened in 2006, but that didn't deter this active spirit from making her presence known.

One of the men who helped with the renovations works there still. We'll call him Benny. This gentleman is a jack-of-all-trades and does a little of everything: handy work, dishwashing, cleaning and the like. Benny spends time in the building by himself frequently and has experienced the presence of the ghost often. He's only seen her once, rushing past him out of a room, but he's felt her presence in the room with him many times, in many different rooms. He inadvertently had a conversation with her one night. It was just before opening time, and there was a problem with one of the swivel bar stools at the upstairs bar. The manager asked Benny to take a look at it. While he was working on the chair, the bartender, a petite young woman, was doing setup for the evening. Since they were both busy, their conversation was light, and Benny was paying more attention to the chair than to the discussion. After a bit, the bartender told Benny that she had finished her preparations and was headed downstairs. About ten minutes passed with Benny still working on the chair before he heard the woman's footsteps coming back upstairs. He heard her walk behind him and then could hear her moving around behind the bar. Still concentrating on the chair, Benny picked up the conversation where they had left off earlier. Shortly thereafter, he heard the young lady call to him from downstairs asking why he was still talking to her when she had told him she was going downstairs. When Benny looked behind the bar to see who had walked by him, there was no one there.

One night, things were pretty slow in the club. There were only about five people at the bar, and both bartenders were out front with them. Benny was in the kitchen, which is situated at the back of the building. He was by himself doing dishes. He had just finished washing and drying a batch of plates and had stacked them up on the counter. Benny stepped out to the front of the restaurant to chat with the bartenders. Five minutes later when he returned to the kitchen the dishes had been spread across the counter. He picked up one of the plates to examine it, and it was still warm from the dishwater, so he knew it was one that he had just washed. As he was looking at the plate, Benny heard footsteps behind him and felt the slight whoosh of air as someone walked briskly by. When he turned to see who it was, there was no one else in the kitchen.

Given the age of the building, the sheer number of different occupants of the building and the plethora of events that have occurred in this section of Main Street, it is impossible to guess who the ghost of 1718 East Main Street may be.

Main Street between Seventeenth and Twenty-fifth Streets is part of the original portion of land outlined when William Byrd II chartered the city of Richmond in 1742. At that time the riverfront tract was just the seed of the city it was to become and most of the plots of land were residential. As trade from the colony proved lucrative, the city grew and Main Street became more commercial as more shops began to open. The first city jail was located at one end of Main Street. The Farmers' Market opened at what is now Seventeenth and Main Streets and has been located there for over two hundred years. Warehouses were built to hold the tobacco and flour awaiting transport to markets all over the world.

Main Street has been the primary witness to the ups and downs of life in the city as it evolves. The 1700 block of Main Street is prone to flooding and the area has been rebuilt many times after a spring flood or a fall hurricane. The worst flood was in 1771, when a spring storm in the mountains caused the James River to rise with little warning to the city. The floodwaters reached forty-five feet above flood stage, washing away people, livestock and homes. In all, 150 people lost their lives. Floods in 1870, 1969 and 1970 also caused widespread damage to the buildings along Main Street.

Main Street was the location of the bread riots during the Civil War, started by women who were fed up with the war and the lack of food for

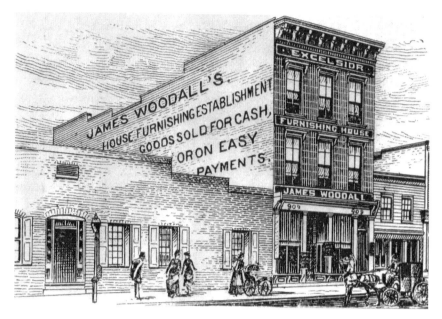

The retail establishments of the time featured the store on the first floor and residential space upstairs. *Courtesy of Virginia State Library.*

their families. The women refused to disperse quietly and instead rallied on Main Street to march against city officials. During the Civil War, many of the area buildings were turned into hospitals. There was so much fighting around Richmond that thousands of soldiers required medical attention. Warehouses offered large interior spaces, perfect for ad hoc medical facilities and prisons. Many warehouses were shut down due to the war and others, owned by Northerners, were simply abandoned. These were commandeered by the Confederate authorities and pressed into service.

After the Civil War, Shockoe Bottom surrounding Main Street continued to grow. With the railroad boom and the opening of Main Street Station, the street was once more a thriving commercial district with many new businesses. The building at 1718 East Main Street originally housed a furniture store. Like its neighbors, the building was built with a tall first story for the shop front on the street and a regular-sized second story, where the family who owned the shop was to live. The property here operated in this manner with a series of stores on the first floor and a corresponding series of families living on the second floor for the first sixty or so years of the twentieth century.

For some unknown reason, it seems that one of the female members of the tenant families of the past has decided to stick around. She remains quiet most of the time when there are guests in the restaurant, but the folks who work there often open up to find evidence that she's still around. Others have said that they can feel her presence when standing in a room. As we found out when we started the Shadows of Shockoe Ghost Tour, ghosts are quite common in this part of town and the folks who work in the restaurant have come to accept her as another one of the things that gives Shockoe Bottom its offbeat charm.

This completes the walking circuit portion of our tour, but since it is a virtual one, we can just flag down a virtual taxi and take a ride up Main Street to visit one last haunted house.

13.

UNFINISHED BUSINESS
AT THE GLASGOW HOUSE

After a short jaunt from Shockoe Bottom through the business district of Richmond, we have the cabbie pull over just across from the Greek Revival house at 1 West Main Street. This well-maintained old house fronted by large magnolia trees is known as the Glasgow House and was the abode of the prominent Richmond novelist Ellen Glasgow. As we get closer and face the front of the house, look at the rightmost window on the second floor: this is the room that the deceased writer is said to haunt.

Ellen Glasgow wrote in *The Past*, "So she isn't real, after all, she is merely a phantom, I found myself thinking, as I fled from the room, and hurried along the hall to the staircase. She is only a ghost, and nobody believes in ghosts any longer. She is something that I know doesn't exist, yet even, though she can't possibly be, I can swear that I have seen her."

Ellen Anderson Gholson Glasgow was born in Richmond in 1873, the ninth of ten children. The Glasgows were a prominent Richmond family, and Ellen was a pretty and popular girl growing up.

Throughout her life, Ellen saw Virginia and the South through the eyes of an enlightened insider, gaining an understanding of both the strengths of Southern culture and of the weaknesses: what she considered to be backward attitudes. Ellen was a proponent of women's rights, and this position is reflected in her work through strong female characters. Through her novels and stories and her written critiques of other works, Ellen encouraged a close look at social morals and an openness to change.

In 1887, Ellen's father, Francis Glasgow, purchased the Greek Revival house at 1 West Main Street. The home would become Ellen's primary residence for the rest of her life. A gracious but fiercely independent person, Ellen was engaged twice, once in her twenties and again in her forties. She did not marry either of the gentlemen, later claiming that she

Ellen Glasgow. *Courtesy of RichmondNowandThen.com.*

never truly loved either of them. In her autobiography, she tells of her only true love, a passionate affair with a mysterious married man, Gerald B., whose real identity has never been discovered. It is believed by many that it was a fear of losing her independence that kept Glasgow from marrying. She stayed active socially throughout her life and feared being thought of as an "old maid," with its connotation of a passionless, pitiable person.

Glasgow's first novel, *The Descendent*, was published in 1897. Over the next fifty years, she wrote eighteen more novels, various short stories and poetry. Included among Glasgow's works are several stories of the supernatural, including *The Shadowy Third*, *The Past* and "Dare's Gift." She was active in the literary community, engaged in discussions and debates with other Richmond authors and pursued friendships with those in positions to help her career and whose work she admired. Ellen worked steadily throughout her career, continuing to write despite a series of heart attacks in her later years. In fact, Miss Ellen was working on a novel when she died at 1 West Main Street in 1945.

According to several accounts related in L.B. Taylor's book *The Ghosts of Richmond and Nearby Environs*, Ellen Glasgow may still be working on that last book to this very day! Several people have reported hearing the sound of clicking typewriter keys coming from Miss Ellen's study. Upon opening the door to the study, the sound ceases, only to start again once the room is vacated. Could Ellen Glasgow still be trying to complete her last great story?

When Miss Ellen lived in the house, she made use of several wall-mounted buzzers to call her servants. Years after her death, some have reported hearing the sound of these servants' buzzers ringing. Interestingly, the buzzers have been disconnected for years.

According to Taylor, Dr. Donald Rhinesmith told of his experience with the spirit of Miss Ellen in a newspaper interview. Dr. Rhinesmith was living in the Glasgow house, using Miss Ellen's former bedroom as his own sleeping quarters. Late one evening, just after he turned out the lights and his head hit the pillow, Rhinesmith heard the sound of footsteps moving around the foot of the bed. He saw no one, but heard the spirit walk over to the window on the east side of the room. After a brief pause, he heard the sound of a foot stomp heavily on the floor as though in frustration. Rhinesmith reasoned that Miss Ellen might have been upset over the destruction of another old Greek Revival house across the street from hers.

One evening on the Shadows of Shockoe tour, one of the guests told our guide a story that backs up Dr. Rhinesmith's theory. The guest stated that he had been a worker on the crew that demolished the Greek Revival

The house at 1 West Main where Ellen Glasgow lived most of her life. *Photo by Jon Hood.*

Ellen Glasgow's tombstone at Hollywood Cemetery. *Photo by Scott Bergman.*

home that stood on the corner of Foushee and East Main Streets just across from the Glasgow house. One morning, the crew crossed the street to take their lunch break in the yard of the Glasgow house. The house was empty at the time, so the crew was surprised to hear a sound coming from inside the house. It was the sound of a woman weeping.

Many people who have spent time in the Glasgow house have reported feeling the presence of a benevolent spirit. A man who lived in the basement of the Glasgow house as a college student reported that on Thanksgiving night of 1965, he entered the empty house and saw a radiant woman standing on the landing of the staircase looking at him. Thinking he recognized the woman, the student glanced over at a picture of Ellen Glasgow that hung on a nearby wall. The dumbfounded man said the resemblance of the picture to the woman on the stairs was uncanny. When he looked again, the woman was gone.

There are two interesting side notes to the Ellen Glasgow story. The first involves Miss Ellen's autobiography, *The Woman Within*. In the book, Glasgow actually states that she felt the presence of ghosts in her house and was "attacked by fear, as by some unseen malevolent power." This raises the interesting possibility of multiple spirits haunting 1 West Main Street.

The other note involves Miss Ellen's pet dogs. Ellen Glasgow was a staunch supporter of the humane treatment of animals. She served as president of the Richmond chapter of the Society for the Prevention of Cruelty to Animals for more than twenty years. Almost all of her novels feature a named dog belonging to a major character. She famously doted upon her own animals, including a well-loved Sealyham terrier named Jeremy. Miss Ellen had Jeremy and another pet dog buried in the yard at 1 West Main Street. Upon her death, Glasgow left instructions for Jeremy and the other dog to be exhumed and reinterred in her plot at Hollywood Cemetery. These orders were carried out and rumor has it that on some nights in Hollywood Cemetery, the two little dogs can be heard barking and playing near Ellen Glasgow's tombstone.

That concludes our virtual tour of some of the haunted places in Richmond. We hope you enjoyed the stories of the Shadows of Shockoe. From here, we invite you to visit one of the many fine establishments in Shockoe Bottom for a meal or a beverage. Here in Richmond's oldest and most haunted neighborhood, your server might just have a ghost story of his or her own to relate.

Please visit us at

www.historypress.net